GREEN

Other Books in the Series:

Colors by Giovanna Ranaldi

Blue by Valentina Zucchi and Viola Niccolai

Red by Valentina Zucchi and Paolo D'Altan

Black by Valentina Zucchi and Francesca Zoboli

White by Valentina Zucchi and Francesca Zoboli

Yellow by Valentina Zucchi and Sylvie Bello

GREEN

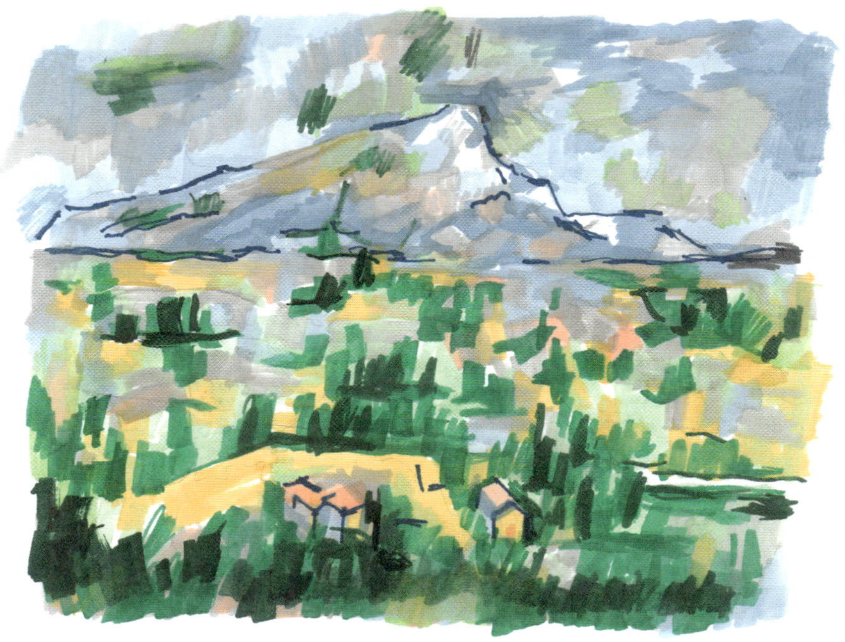

BY VALENTINA ZUCCHI
AND ANGELA LEON

Translated from the Italian
by Katherine Gregor

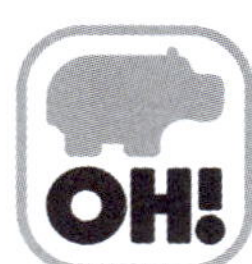

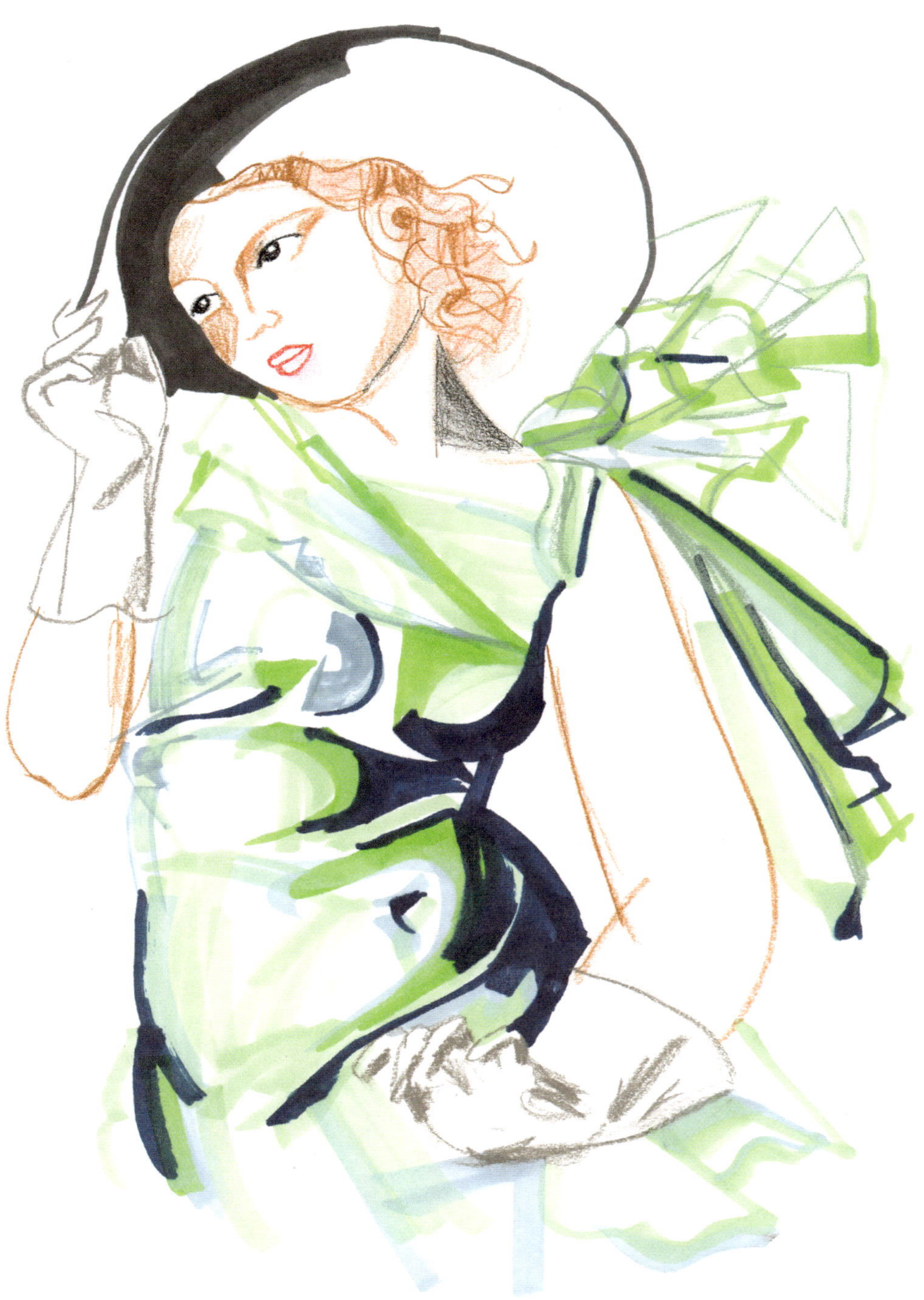

Tamara de Lempicka, *Girl in a Green Dress*, 1930-1931, Centre Pompidou, Paris

CONTENTS

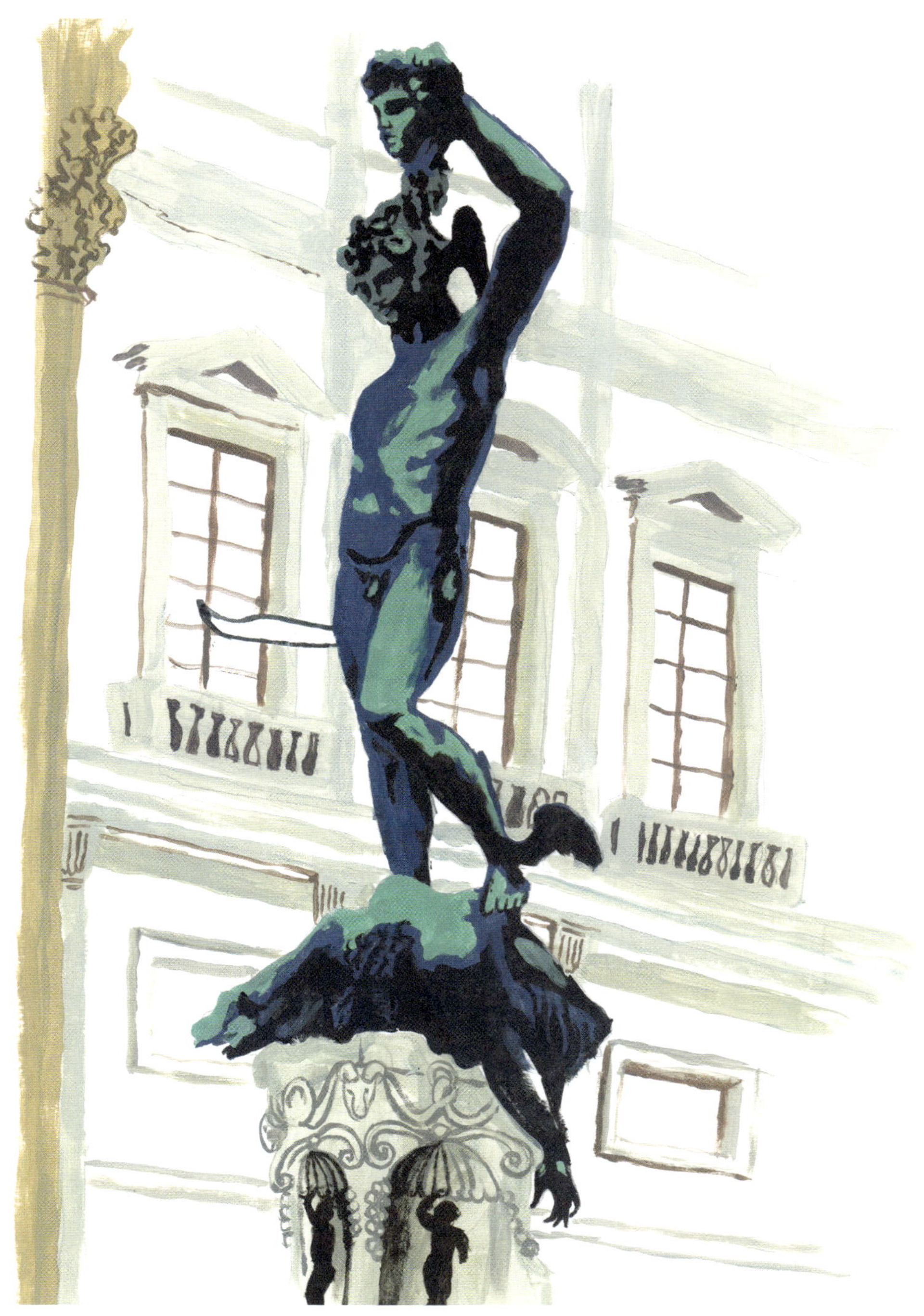

Benvenuto Cellini, *Perseus with the Head of Medusa*, 1545–1554, Piazza Signoria, Florence

LIFE AND ABUNDANCE

Since the dawn of time, green has been a sign of life, fertility, and abundance. It has offered the promise of food and well-being which the Earth, mother of all living creatures, has the power to bestow. It is no wonder that for the ancients, green was associated with other words that were connected with strength, life, spring, and even virtue. Nowadays, green still imparts energy, relaxes, refreshes, cleanses, and heals. Let us look together at how artists have viewed it up to now.

Throughout the book, you will find spaces to extend drawings, try out suggested exercises, make your own sketches or notes and write your impressions about what you see, notice and think. Make sure you always have a notebook with you so you never lose a creative idea or impression.

THE COLOR OF NATURE

Green ultimately belongs to nature: meadows, woods, and fields but also waters, streams, and seas. Human beings have always enjoyed plunging into and abandoning themselves to this immense green, so much so that – thanks to the magic of painting – they decided to take it into their homes. And so monarchs over the years have imagined bringing gardens and meadows to life on their bedroom walls, as illustrated by the wonderful, flowery garden that Livia, the wife of the Roman Emperor Augustus, had painted in one of the rooms in her villa, where the walls are green with trees, rich with flowers and fruit, surrounded by the twittering of birds and the sound of the wind. In fact, there are 69 kinds of bird and 23 kinds of plant, to be exact! Can you recognize any of them?

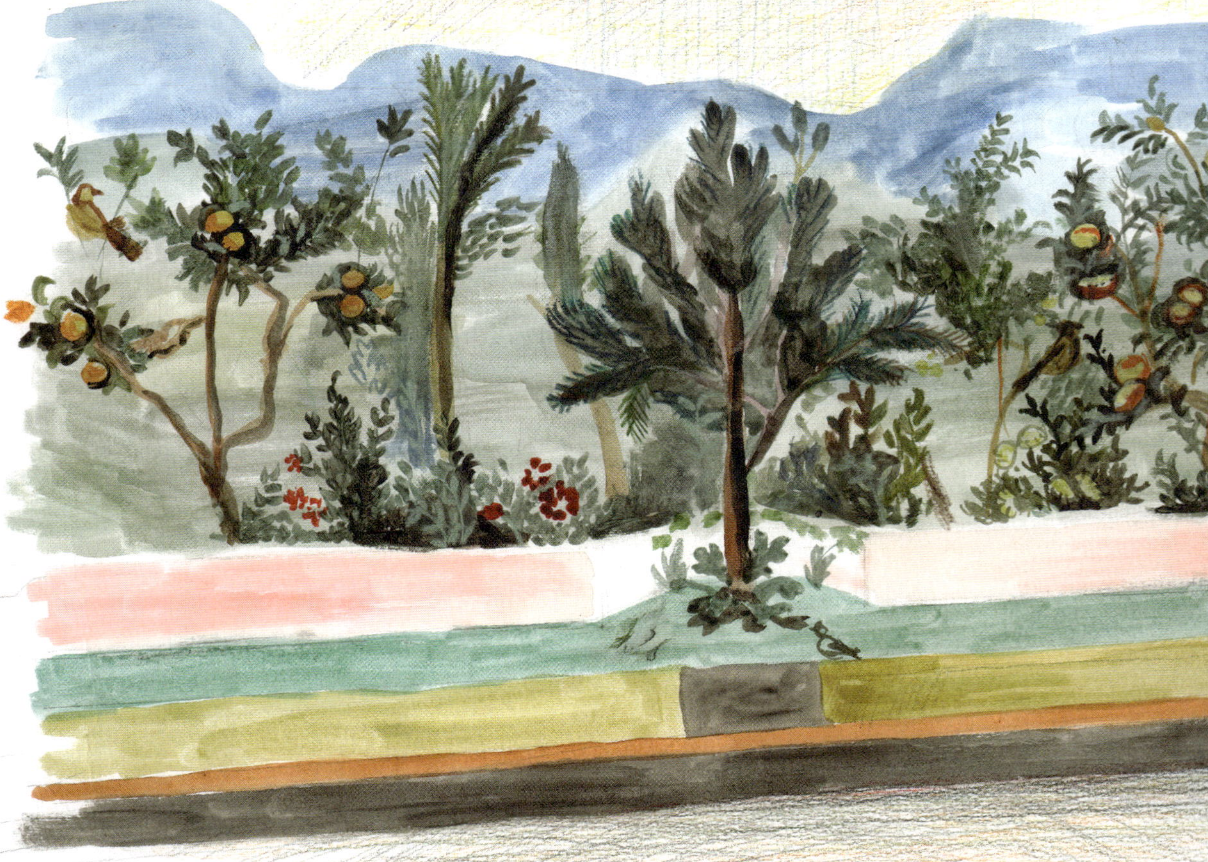

Garden in Flower (40–20 BCE), Villa of Livia at Prima Porta, Rome

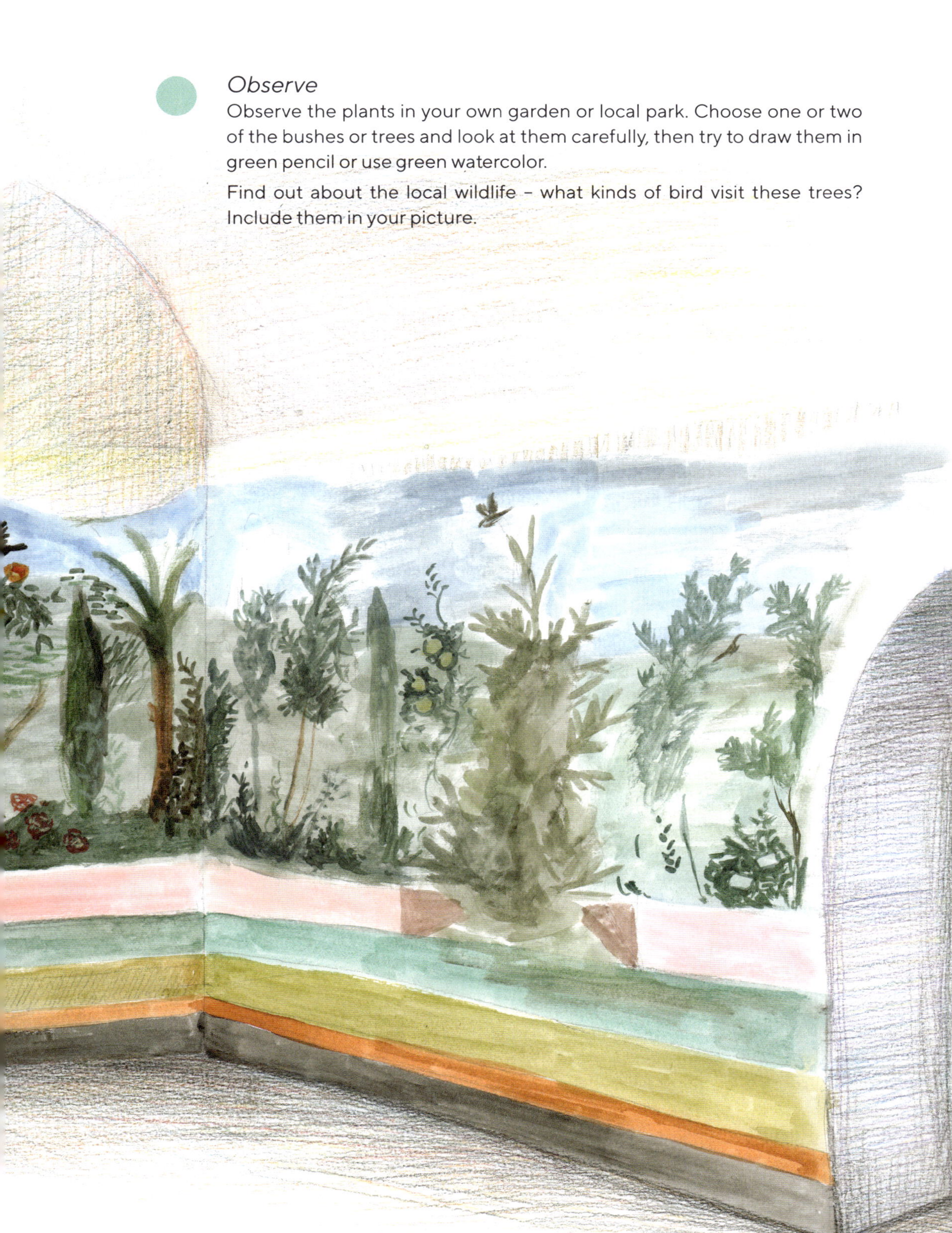

Observe

Observe the plants in your own garden or local park. Choose one or two of the bushes or trees and look at them carefully, then try to draw them in green pencil or use green watercolor.

Find out about the local wildlife – what kinds of bird visit these trees? Include them in your picture.

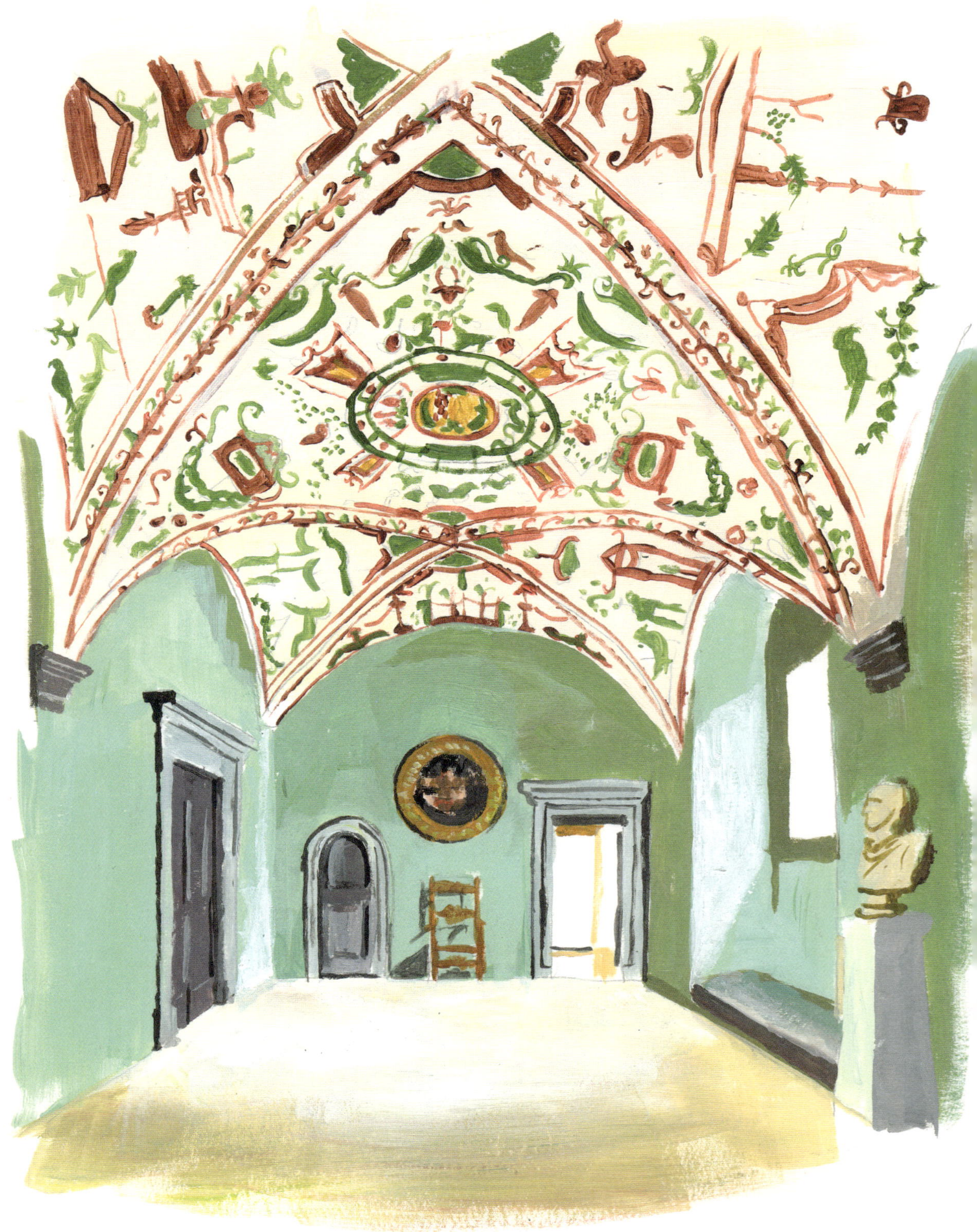

INDOOR EXOTIC GARDEN

Traveling through time, we reach the Green Room of Duchess Eleonora. There are luxuriant landscapes on the walls; above our heads, decorations made of plants, flowers, and fruits (including lemons and limes, which Eleonora loved), brightened by real and fantastical animals. Among these there are also a few exotic parrots that were brought to Florence from Africa and from a distant land that had only just been explored by Europeans: America.

Fantastical Animals
Use the space below to draw your own fantastical animal, or perhaps a brightly colored parrot.

Ridolfo del Ghirlandaio, *Green Room*, 1542–1545, Palazzo Vecchio, Florence

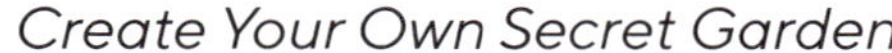

Create Your Own Secret Garden

In order to create your secret garden, you need a few large sheets of white paper, pencils, felt-tip pens, watercolors or crayons. Don't make your pieces of paper too large or they will be difficult to manage.

Now plan a two-dimensional garden on your paper. You can draw trees, flowers, plants, a wood, or a meadow. Draw inspiration from nature around you or from paintings you like by searching online. Do not forget to add to your garden's hidden residents, like insects, birds or other animals. Once you have finished your creation, hang it on your bedroom walls. This way you will be able to imagine that you are in a garden even when you don't want to go outside.

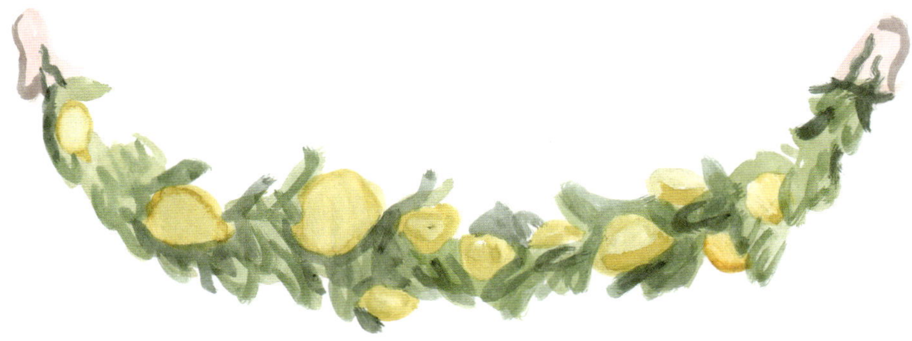

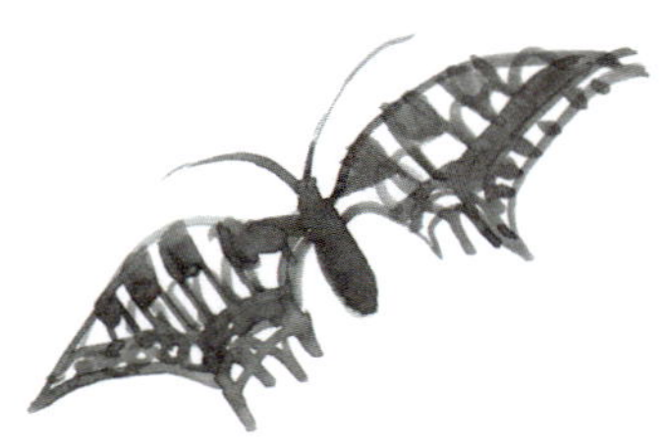

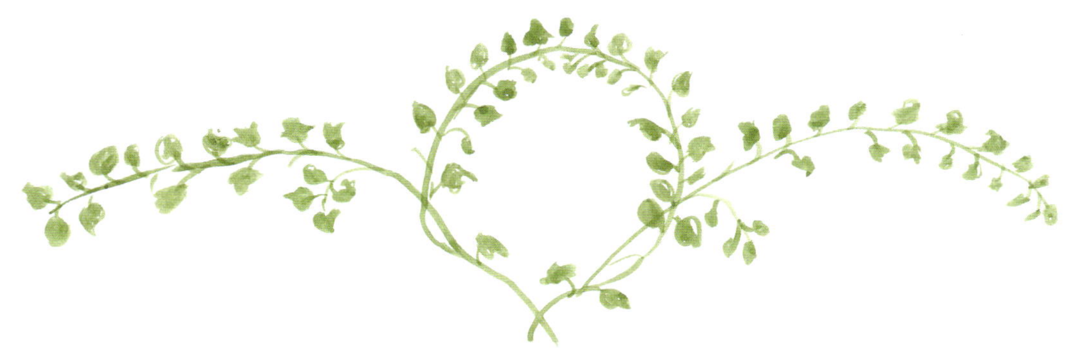

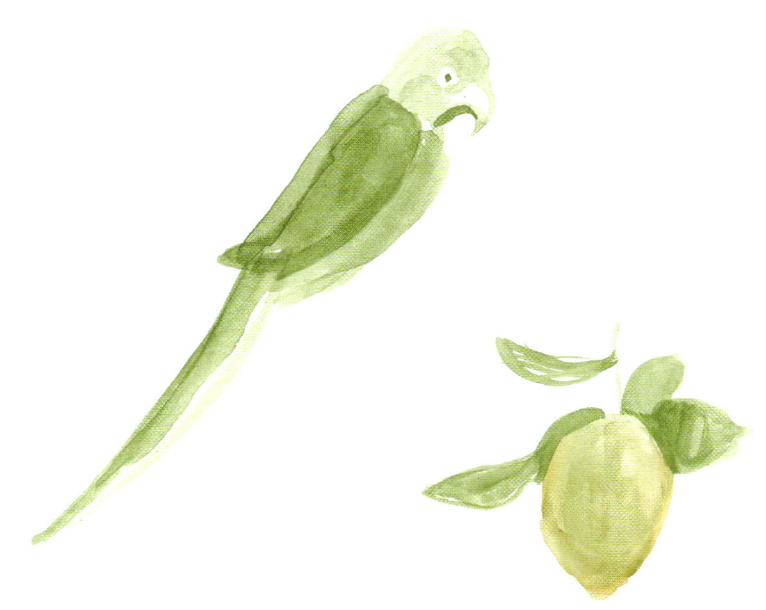

A FOREST OF GREENS

Now you have begun to look with an artist's eye at the greens all around you, try to replicate them on paper by making your own color palette.

Green is not a primary color: it is made from mixing yellow and blue and, depending on the quantities used of both, the green will be more or less dark, more towards blue or towards yellow. In order to obtain more shades, you can add a hint of white, brown, black, or red. This is the magic of colors: artists know this well and play with the endless possibilities of their palettes. Experiment with your watercolors and see how many distinct greens you can create, varying the proportions of blue and yellow, and adding black, white, blue, brown, red, or other colors to make palette of greens.

Go out into the open air and carefully observe the plants around you – can you discover even more variations? You will need to mix many different colors in order to reproduce all the wealth of tones you see. When you are mixing, always start with the lightest color and add the darker shades a very little at a time so you are in control of the mixing process.

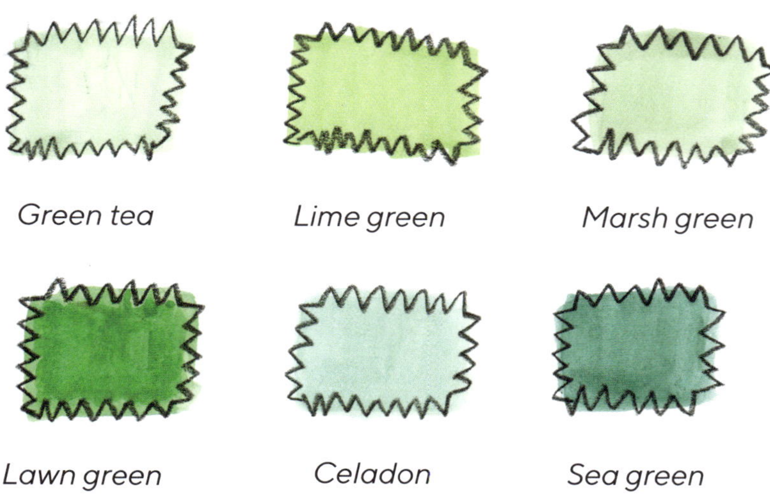

Green tea

Lime green

Marsh green

Lawn green

Celadon

Sea green

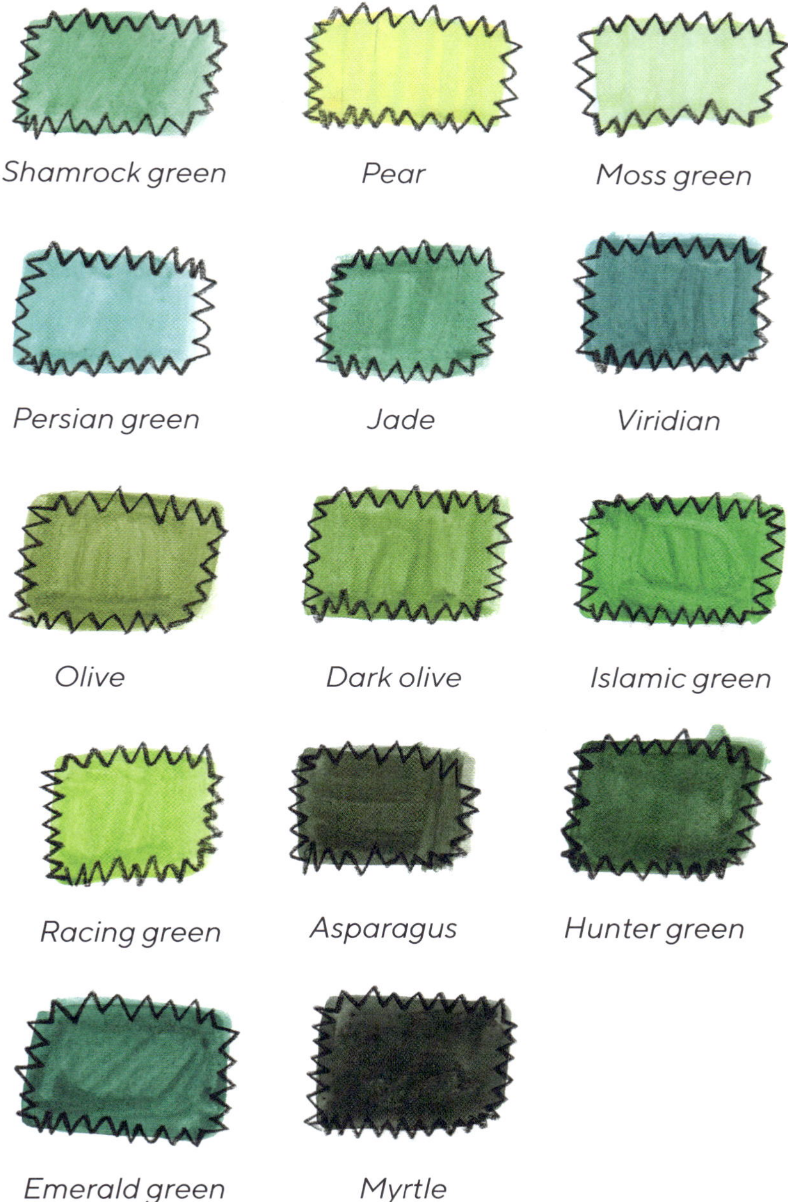

Shamrock green
Pear
Moss green
Persian green
Jade
Viridian
Olive
Dark olive
Islamic green
Racing green
Asparagus
Hunter green
Emerald green
Myrtle

THE WATERLILIES AT GIVERNY

Artists have always loved the green in nature. Therefore, in the 19th century, when they emerged from their studios to paint in the open air, nature triumphed in their work. Impressionists – called that because they focused on conveying in their paintings feelings and impressions of the moment – liked natural landscapes very much and made them the central feature of their work.

One of these artists adored the waterlilies and flowers in his own garden, and painted them innumerable times over the span of about thirty years – at a thousand moments and from a thousand viewpoints, playing with light and the reflection of the water, reproducing on canvas the extraordinary shades of green nature can generate. He did not stop even when his eyesight began to fail. This French artist was Claude Monet and his garden at Giverny, west of Paris, is now open to the public.

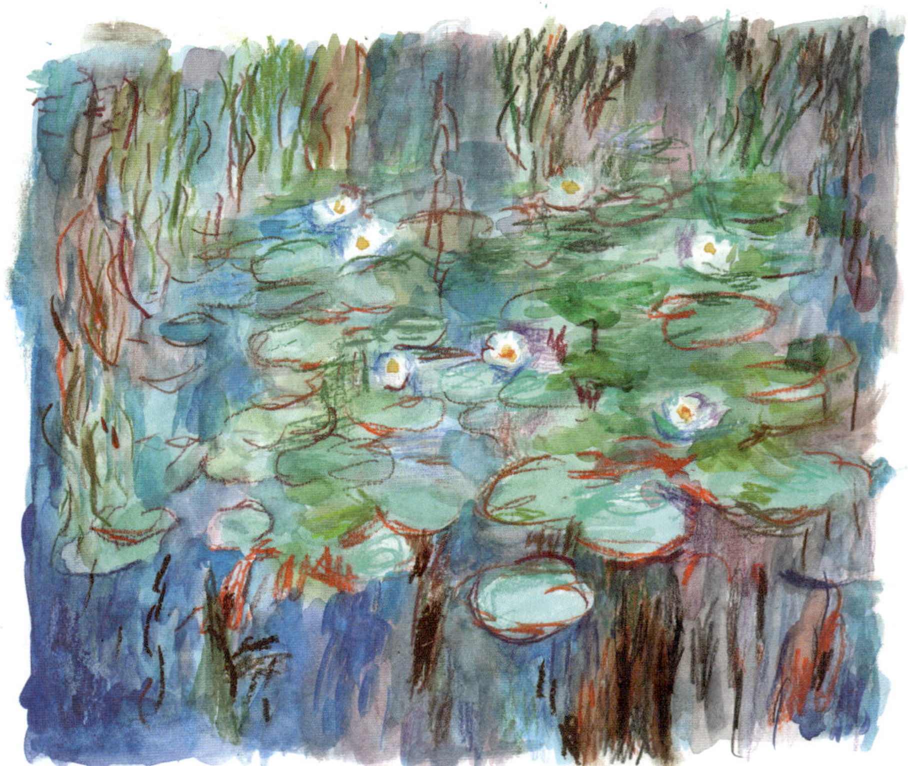

Claude Monet, *Nymphéas*, 1916–1919, Musée d'Orsay, Paris

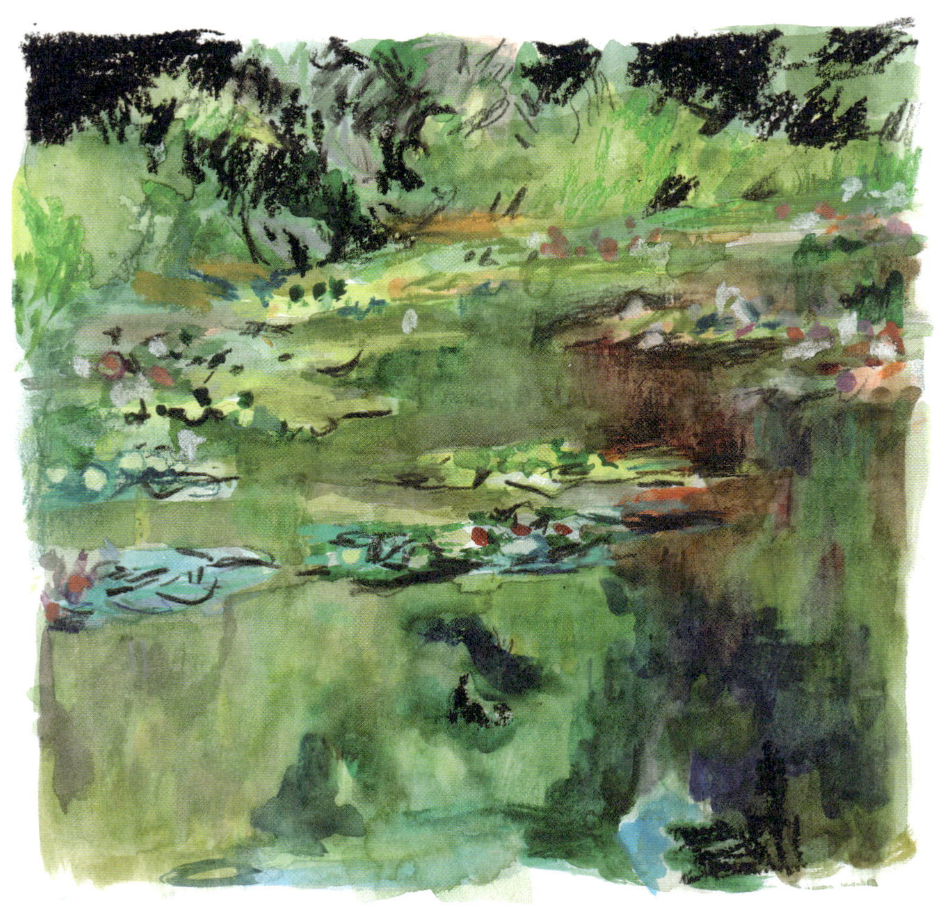

Claude Monet, *Le Bassin des Nymphéas*, 1904, Denver Art Museum

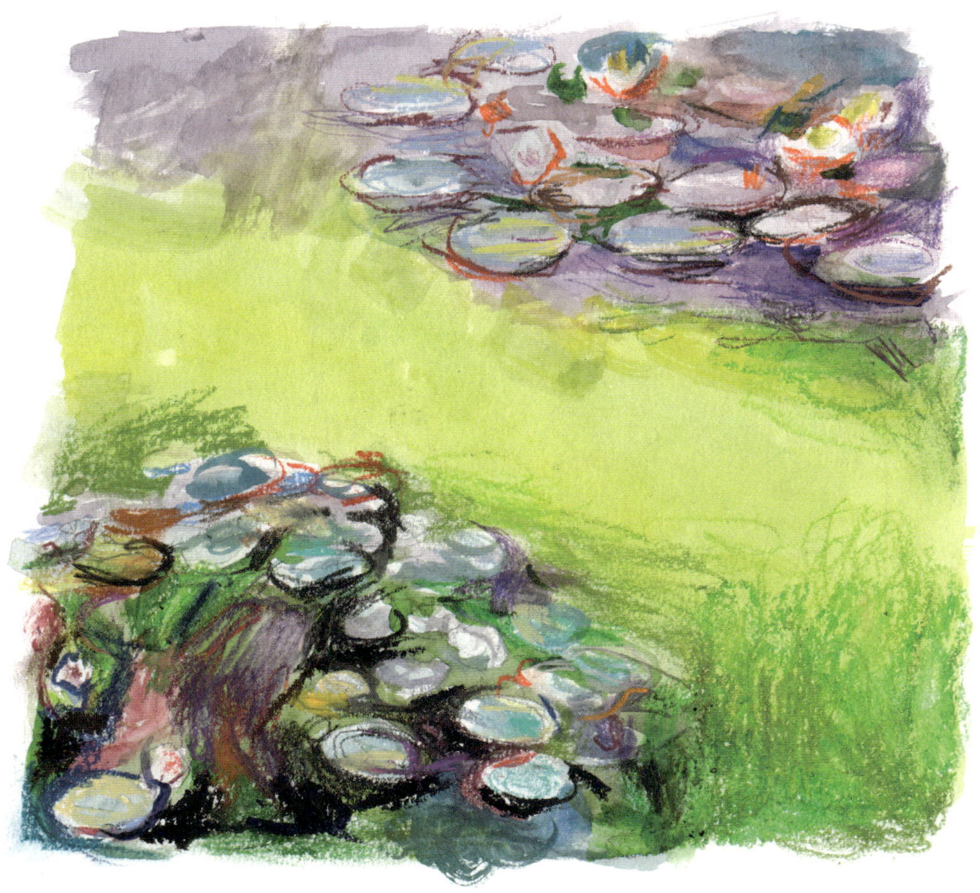

Claude Monet, *Water Lilies*, 1914, Musée Marmottan, Paris

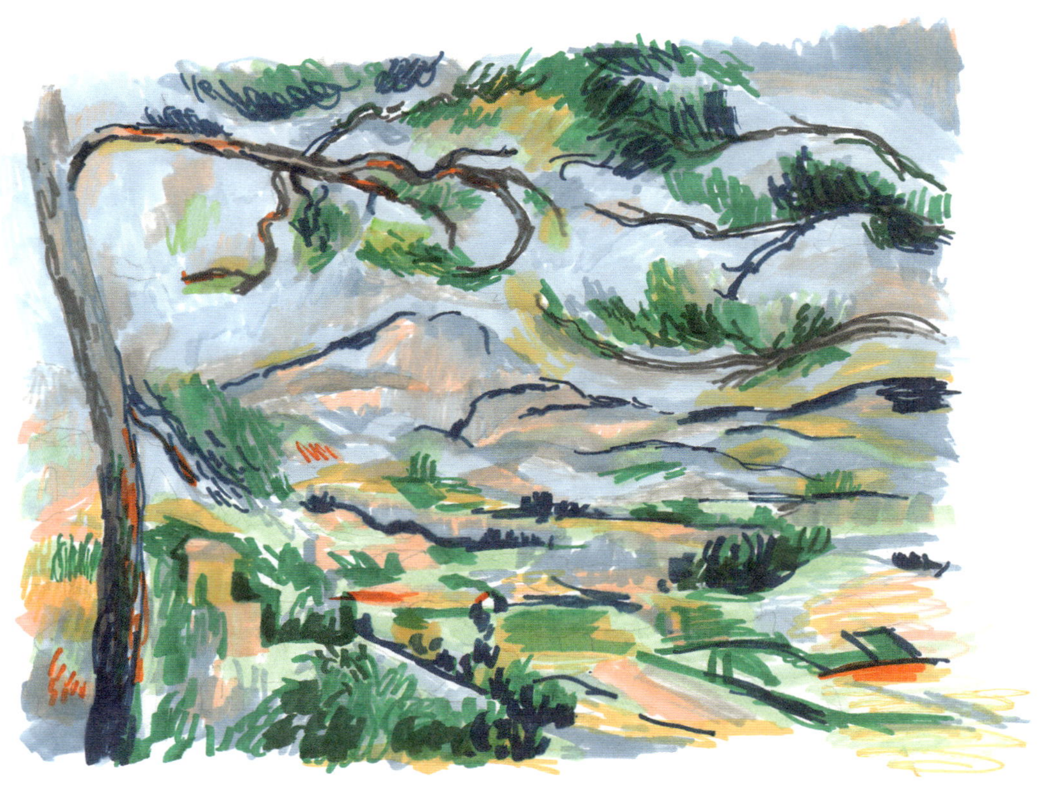

Paul Cézanne, *Mont Sainte-Victoire with Large Pine*, 1887, Courtauld Institute Galleries, London

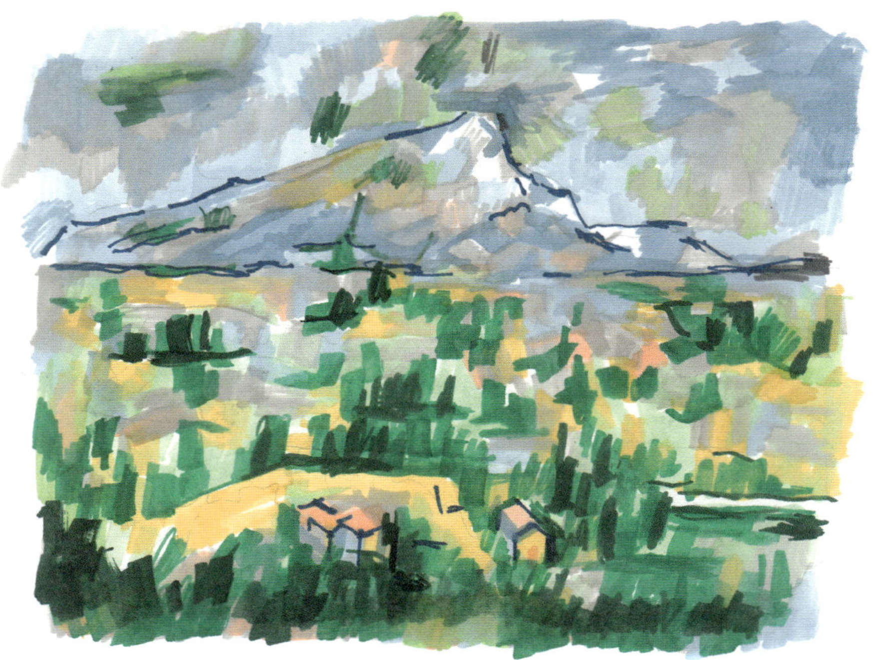

Paul Cézanne, *Mont Sainte-Victoire*, 1902–1906, Metropolitan Museum of Art, New York

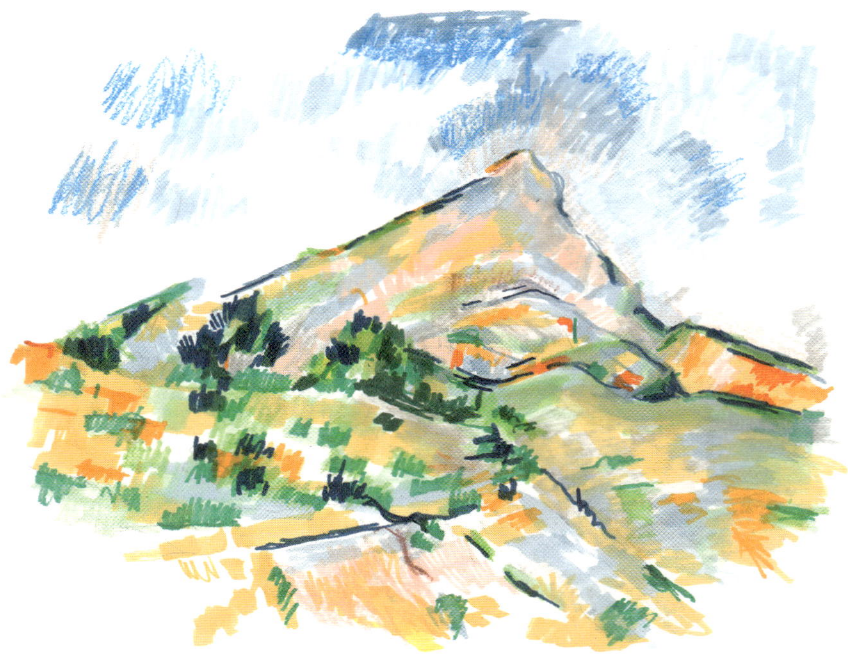

Paul Cézanne, *Mont Sainte-Victoire*, 1897–1898, Hermitage Museum, Saint Petersburg

Watching Through the Seasons

Choose a landscape that you can visit regularly and that you enjoy. Watch it and paint it throughout the year, in different lights and weather conditions. How do these factors change the colors you see and reproduce, especially the predominant greens?

EXOTIC AND ENCHANTED

Magic and mysterious is nature as imagined by another French painter, Henri Rousseau, who loved going to the botanical gardens and the natural history museum of his city, Paris, to draw inspiration and create an exotic, enchanted world of luxuriant jungle. Even though he had never been to a jungle in real life, the artist dreamt of extraordinary wild forests that took over space and surrounded every living being. He painted them with precision, giving anyone looking at them the notion of a magical place, suspended in time and space.

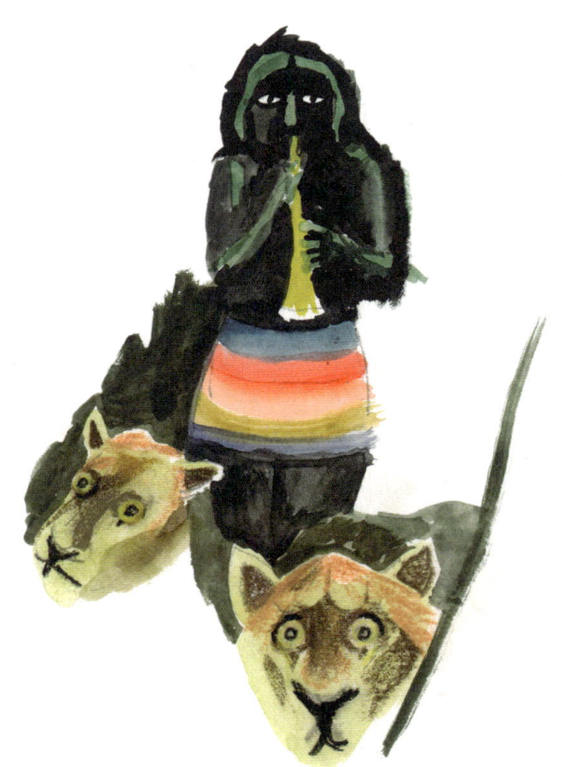

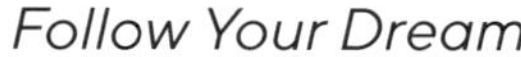

Follow Your Dream

What would your dream jungle be like? Imagine the landscape of somewhere you have never been and create it on your paper in whatever medium you prefer. Take green as your central color but work with contrast and tone to express the variety of life in the dense jungle. This is a dreamscape so you can introduce as much fantasy as you wish.

Growing the Jungle

Using your favorite greens, color in the jungle around the figures in this painting, the setting of which may have been suggested to the painter in a dream. What is the effect of combining the dream images and the real?

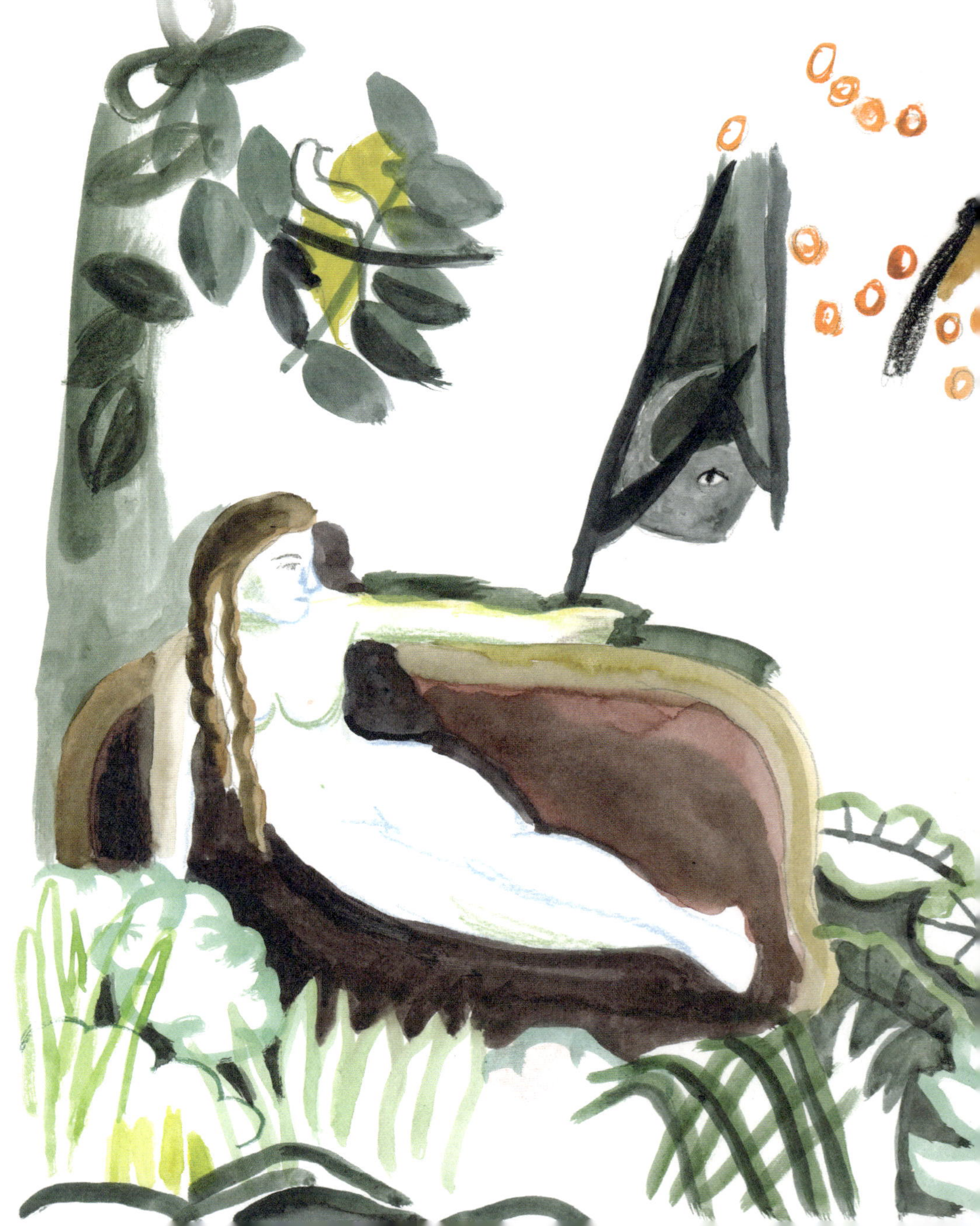

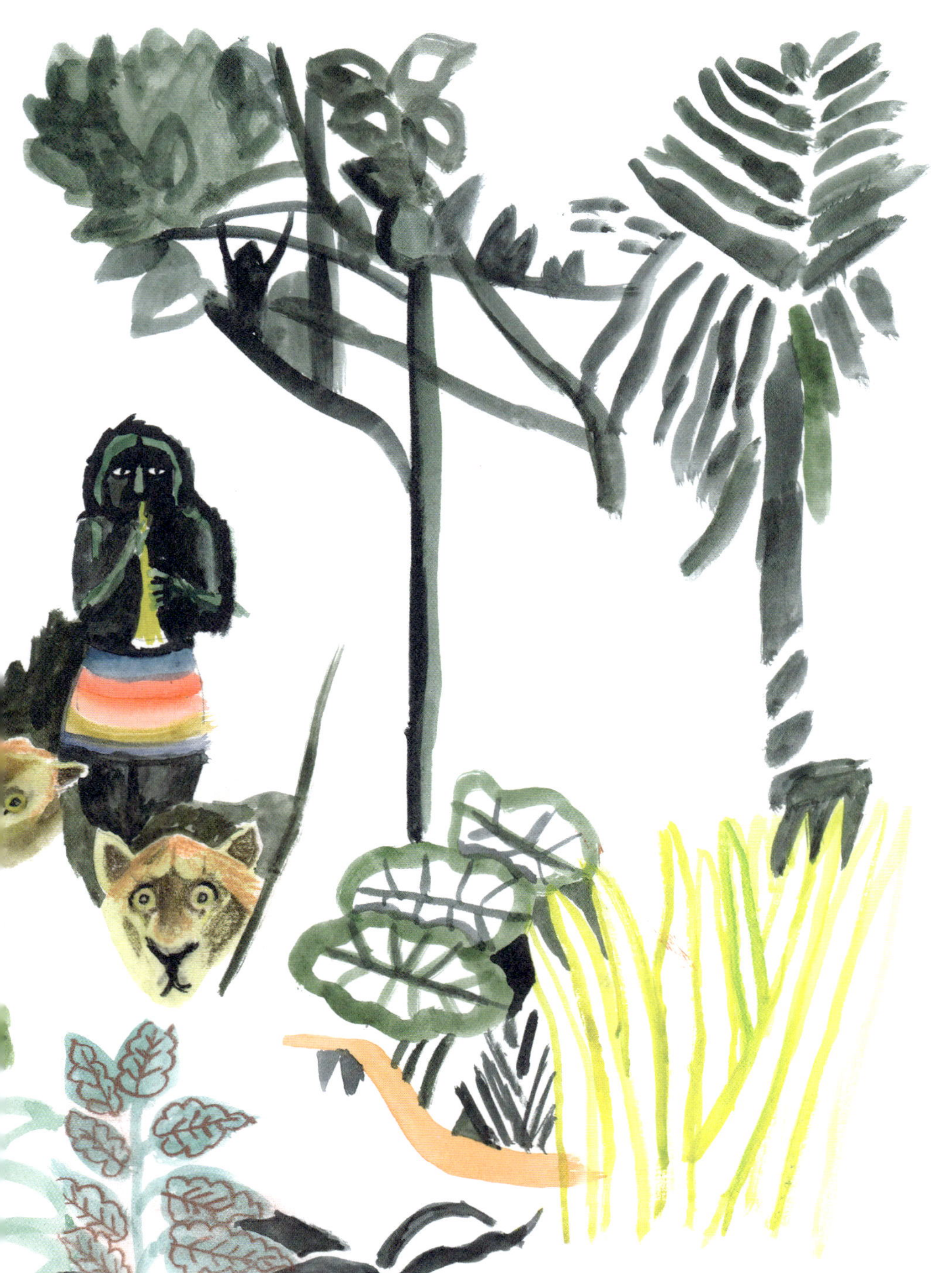

Henri Rousseau, *The Dream*, 1910, Museum of Modern Art, New York

A SNAKE IN THE GRASS

The green of nature, however, may also conceal dangers. Snakes, for instance, are perfectly camouflaged amongst the leaves and branches of the forest floor, and can become almost invisible.

In ancient Greek myths, we encounter a monster woman with snakes instead of hair: Medusa. Anyone who met her gaze would be turned to stone. One day, Perseus, a brave hero, succeeded in cutting off her head. Following the advice of the goddess Athena, he walked backwards towards her, watching her reflection in a polished shield.

There is a sculpture of the hero Perseus in Florence: the lifeless body of the monster lies at the young man's feet as he proudly holds up the severed head. The statue has a greenish color: this is because it is made of bronze, a metal used by humans since the Bronze Age which, when in contact with air and water, tends to form a green patina. The greens produced in this way by bronze and also copper are actually the result of a chemical reaction called oxidation. Some contemporary artists, like Anselm Kiefer, have used this phenomenon to illustrate the effect of nature and the passing of time in their works.

Benvenuto Cellini, *Perseus with the Head of Medusa*,
1545–1554, Piazza Signoria, Florence

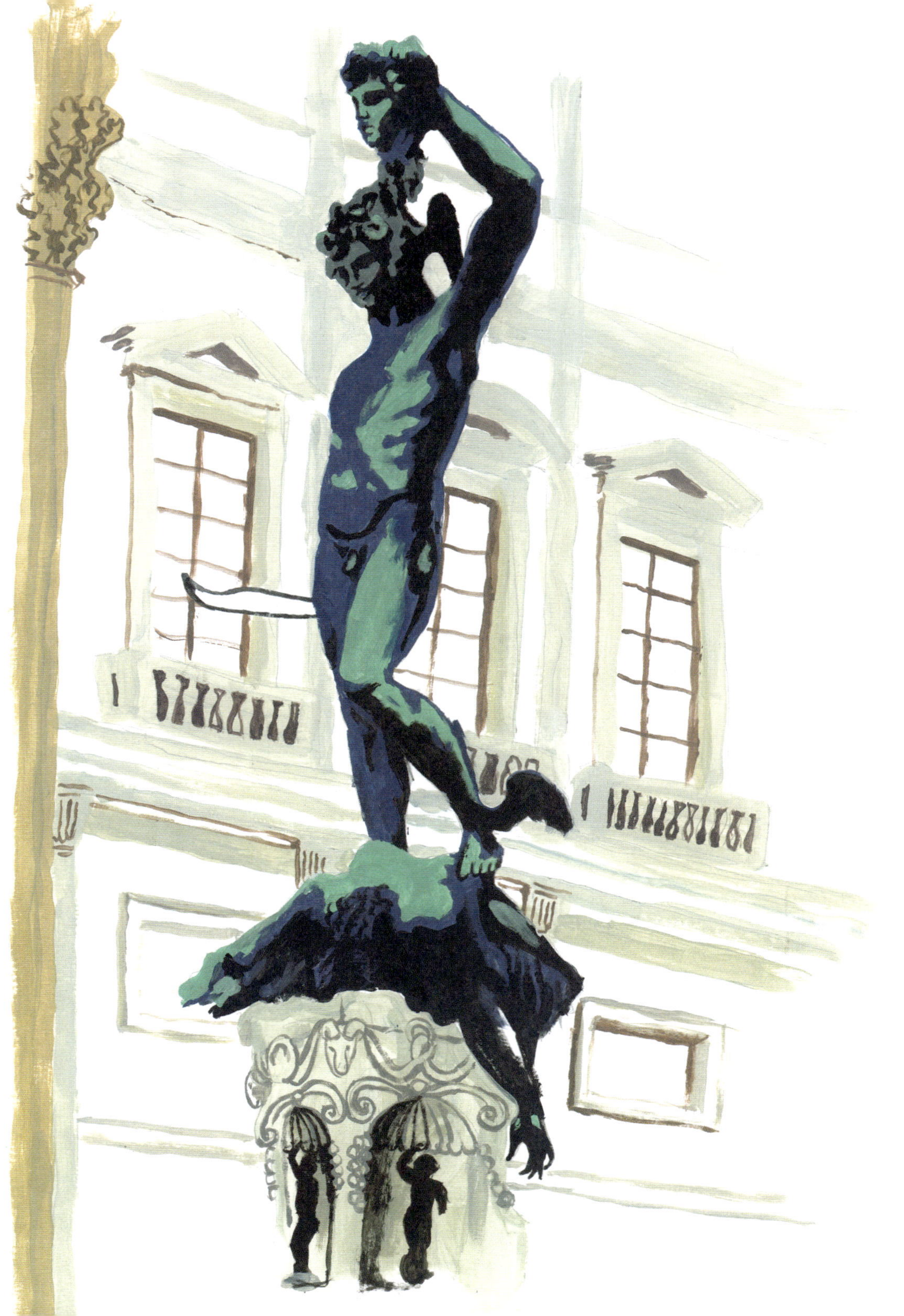

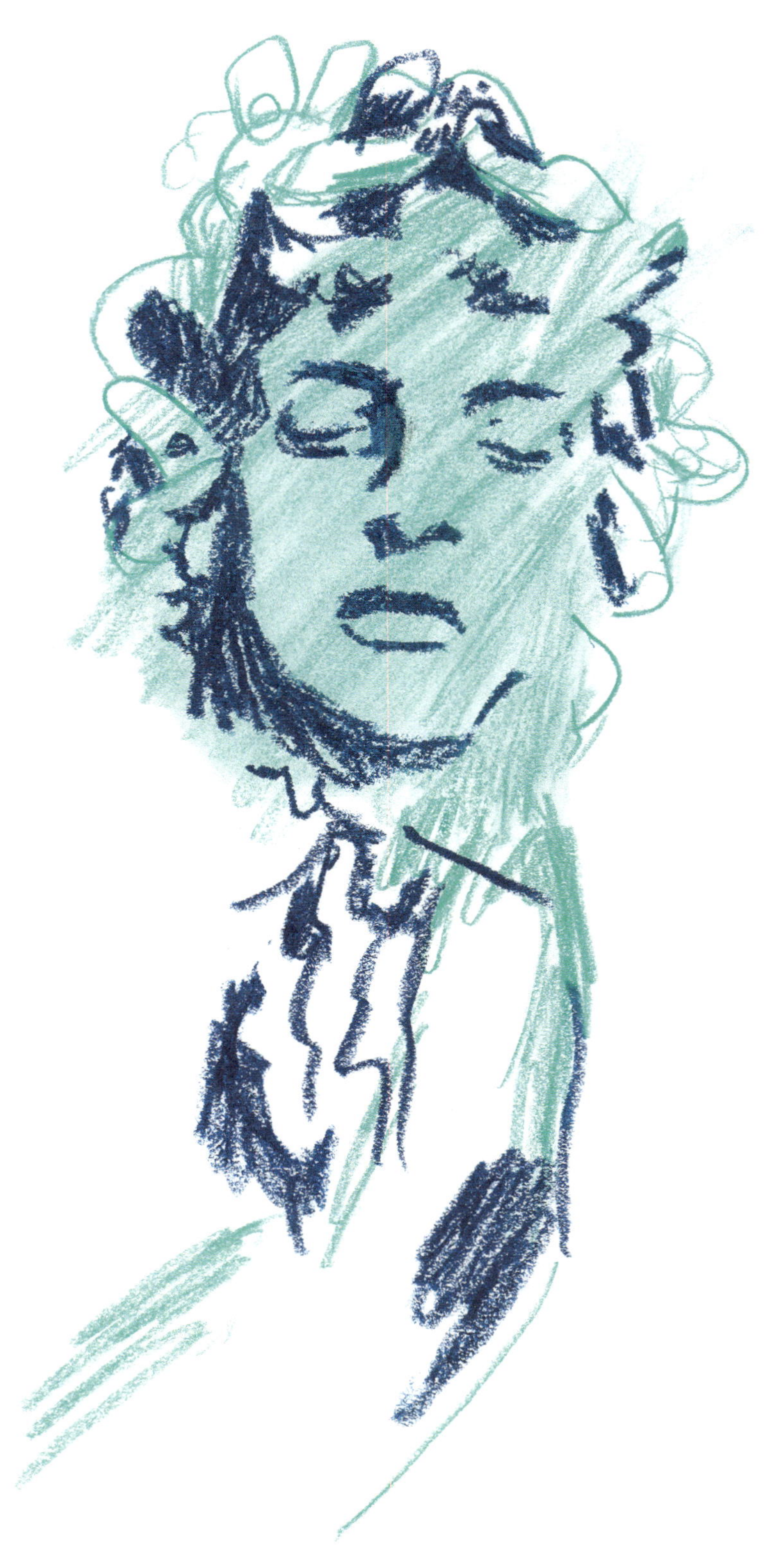

Medusa

Once a beautiful goddess, Medusa's face and hair were transformed by Athena, making them so hideous that no one could look at her without being literally petrified.

What do you think Medusa looked like to be so terrifying? Using green pencils or watercolors, draw a representation of the head of Medusa as though in oxidized copper or bronze.

REALISM AND OBSERVATION

How did Cellini manage to represent snakes so perfectly? One theory is that he got the idea from the drawings of naturalists who, during those same years, were focusing on depicting with precision the world's plants, animals, and minerals. One of the best among them was Jacopo Ligozzi. His books on plants were called herbaria and were made by reproducing herbs, leaves, and flowers in minute detail and in the original colors, but also preserving individual dried specimens. One famous herbarium is by the Bologna-born Ulisse Aldrovandi who worked on the project for many years, managing to collect an vast number of "natural things", including herbs and plants. He wrote with pride that six months would not be enough to visit his extraordinary museum.

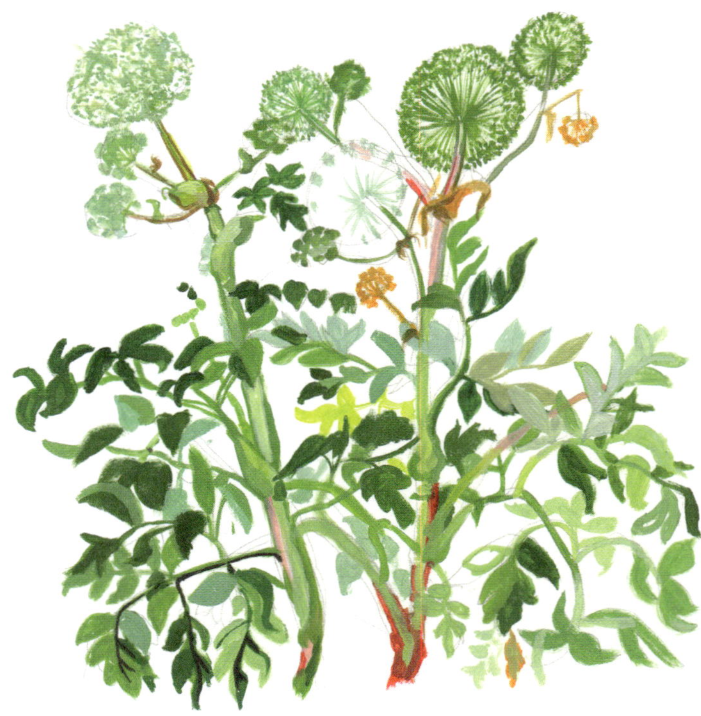

Jacopo Ligozzi, *Drawings, Gabinetto disegni e stampe degli,* Uffizi, Florence

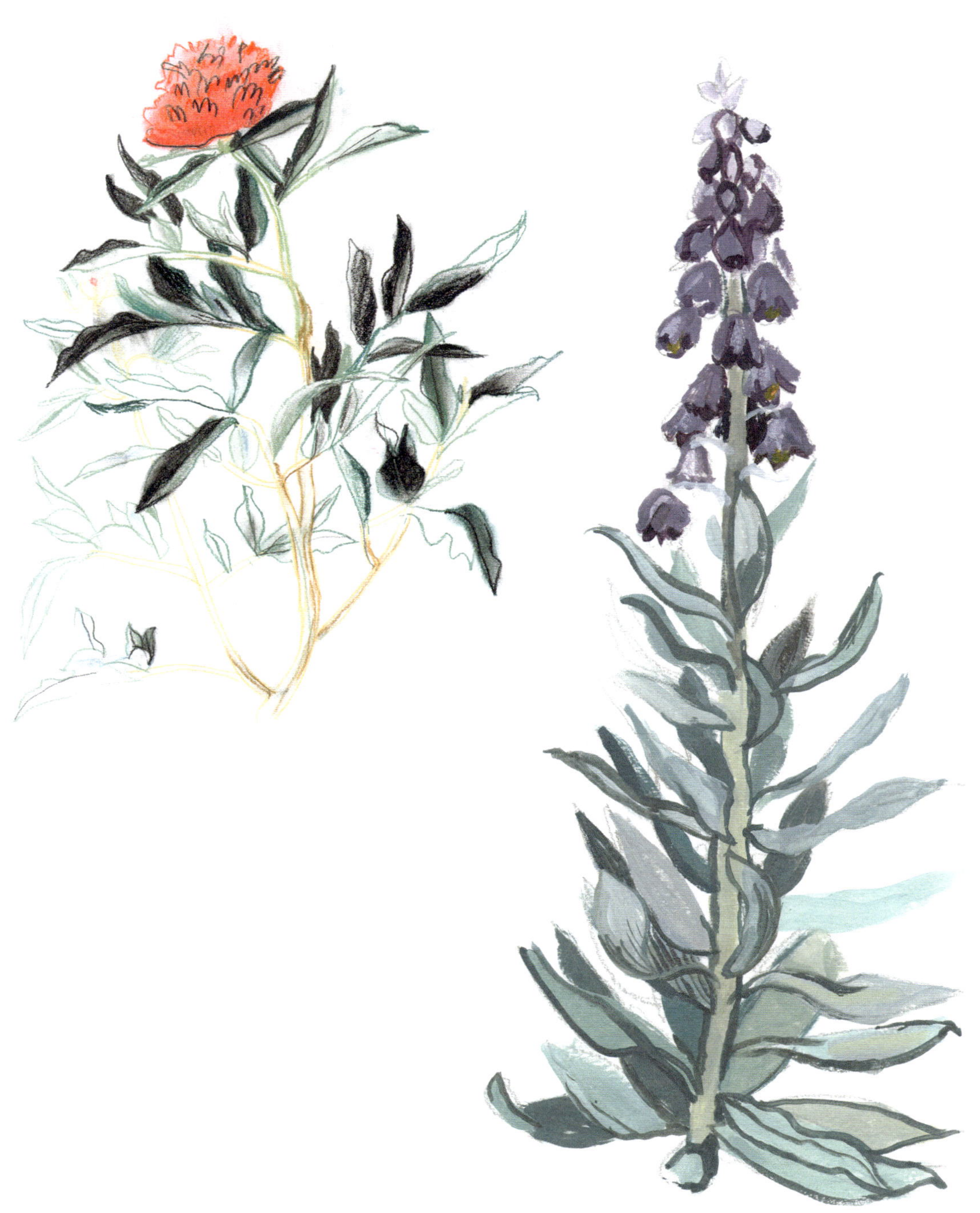

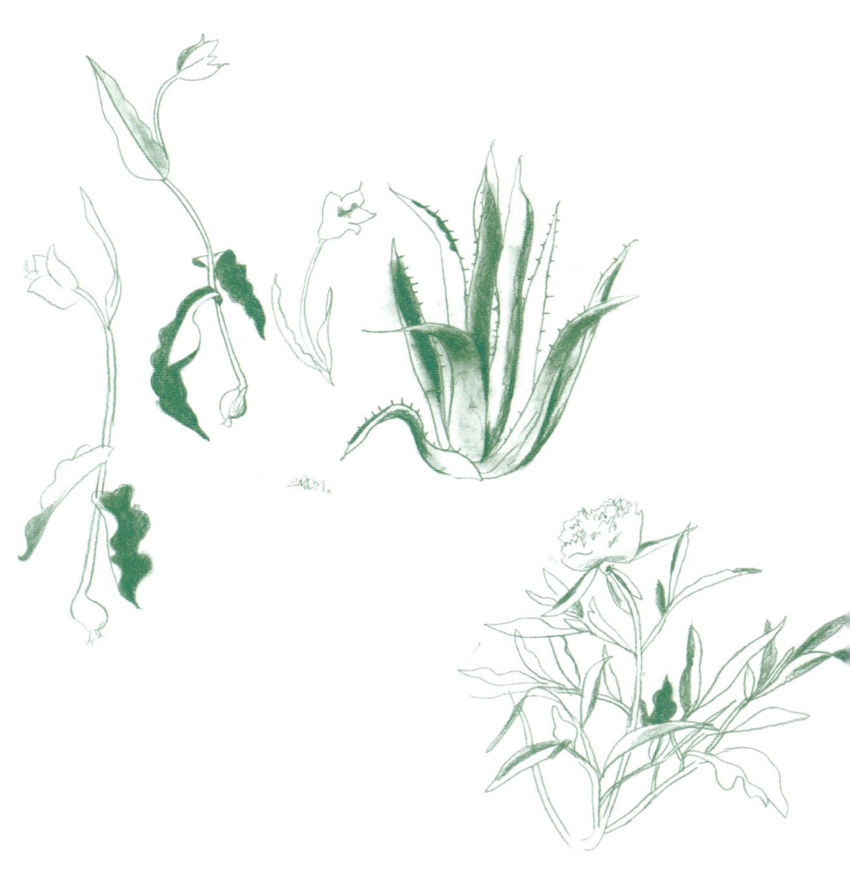

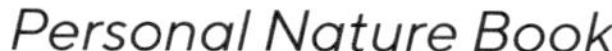

Personal Nature Book

In order to create your own big book of nature, all you need is a notebook and a keen eye. You can jot down your daily observations in it and document them with your own drawings, using any media you prefer. You could also include pressed flowers or cut-out pictures, illustrations and photos.

THE STRUGGLE BETWEEN GOOD AND EVIL

Perhaps because they have always been associated with snakes and lizards, dragons are also often depicted as green. Scary and very powerful creatures with skin as hard as armor, they are also capable of spitting fire. A wonderful presence in fantasy novels and poems, movies, frescoes, and paintings, they are usually paired with some hero or other ready to face them bravely in a battle that is symbolic of good and evil, and in which the good always prevails. This is the case in the story of the knight George – who later became a saint – who, no sooner did he hear of a princess delivered to a terrible dragon than he engaged in battle, stabbed the monster with his spear and freed the girl.

Saint George is probably the most famous slayer of dragons, but there are plenty more, including Saint Michael and Saint Margaret. This painting by Uccello depicts the moment when the knight conquers the beast.

Paolo Uccello, *Saint George and the Dragon*, 1456, National Gallery, London

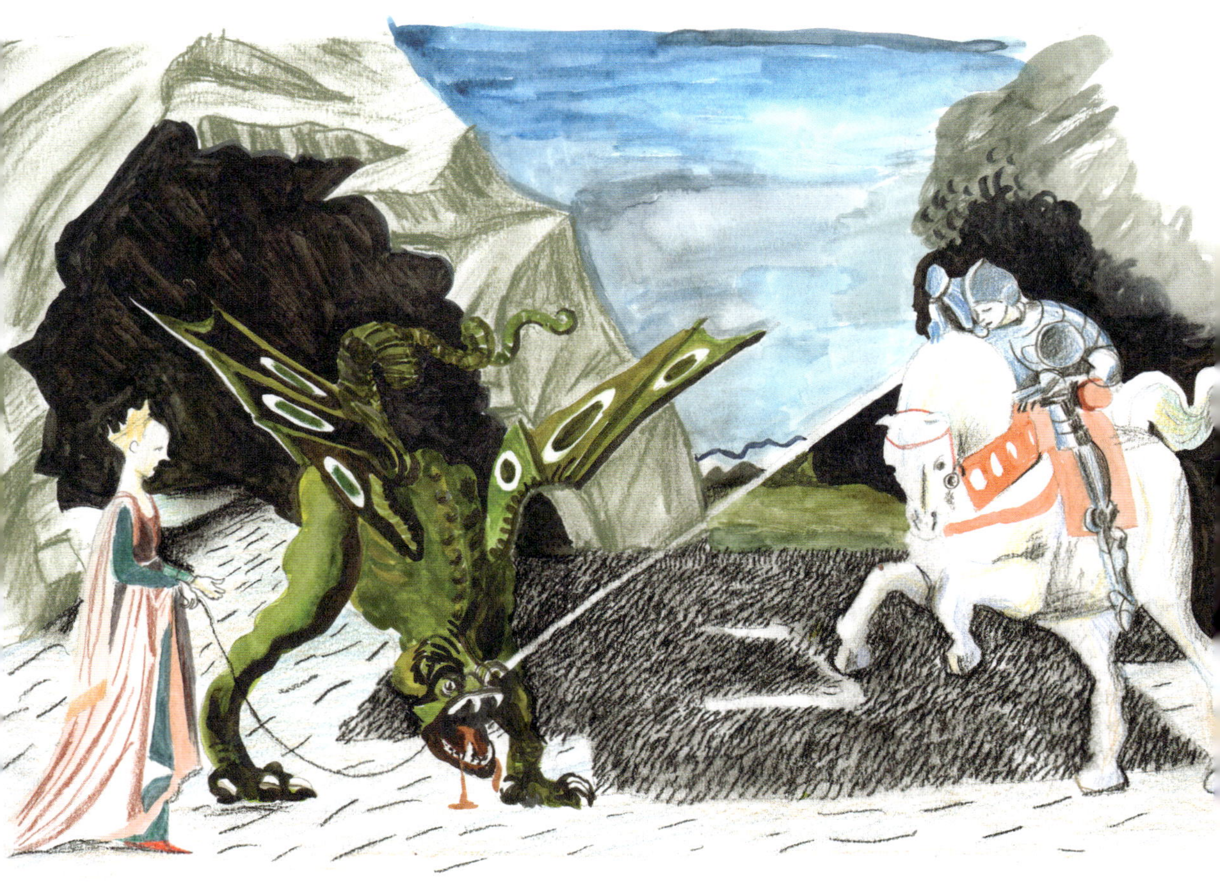

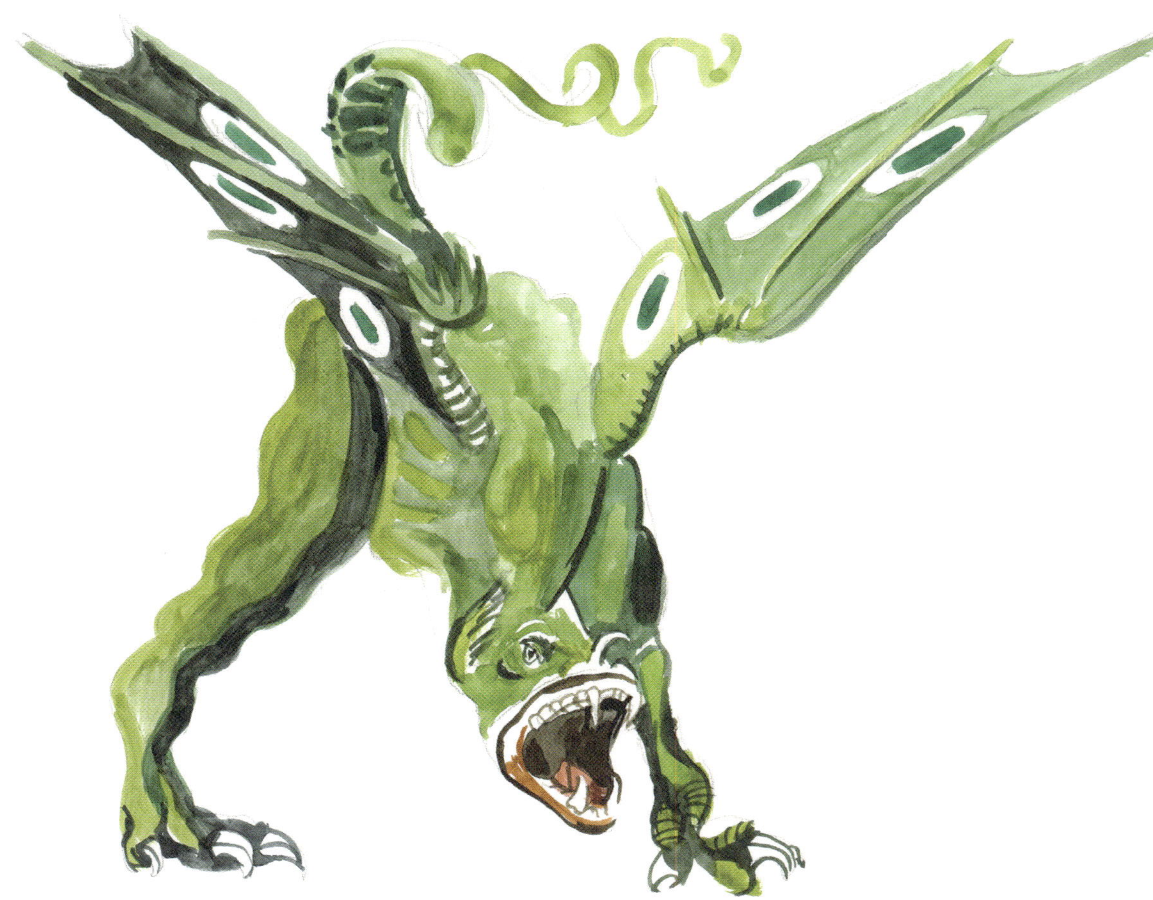

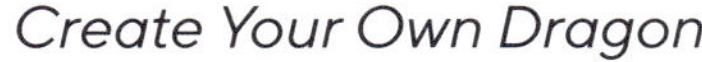

Create Your Own Dragon

In order to draw your own version of a dragon, draw inspiration from the dragon in Uccello's painting. You could also search online or in the library for other magnificent paintings devoted to these saints and their dragon-slaying exploits, or to dragons in general. Think about the dragon's weapons: claws, teeth, tail, and fiery breath. How does the animal protect itself? Where are the weaknesses that the knight can exploit in order to defeat the creature?

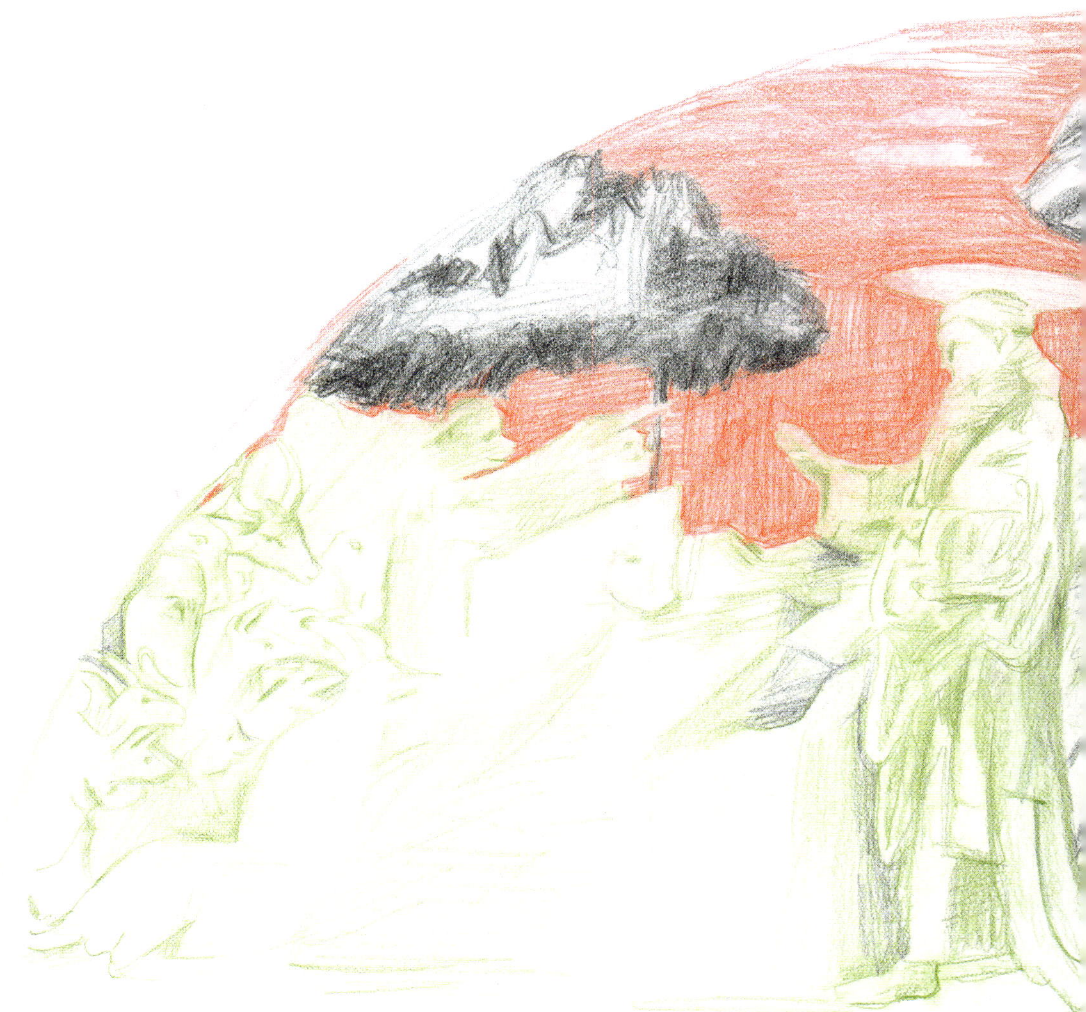

FRESCOES OF THE CREATION

Also by the same artist, Uccello, and his colleagues is a peculiar series of frescoes that gave its name to the place for which it was created: the Green Cloister in Santa Maria Novella, in Florence. The series has a special characteristic: everything has a green hue. The reason for this is not precisely known but what we do now know is that the artists did not, as previously believed, use herbs and juices from leaves and plants but a "green earth" (*terra verde*). The paintings tell the story of the creation of the world and the events surrounding the first humans, which is why one of the first scenes represents God's creation of animals.

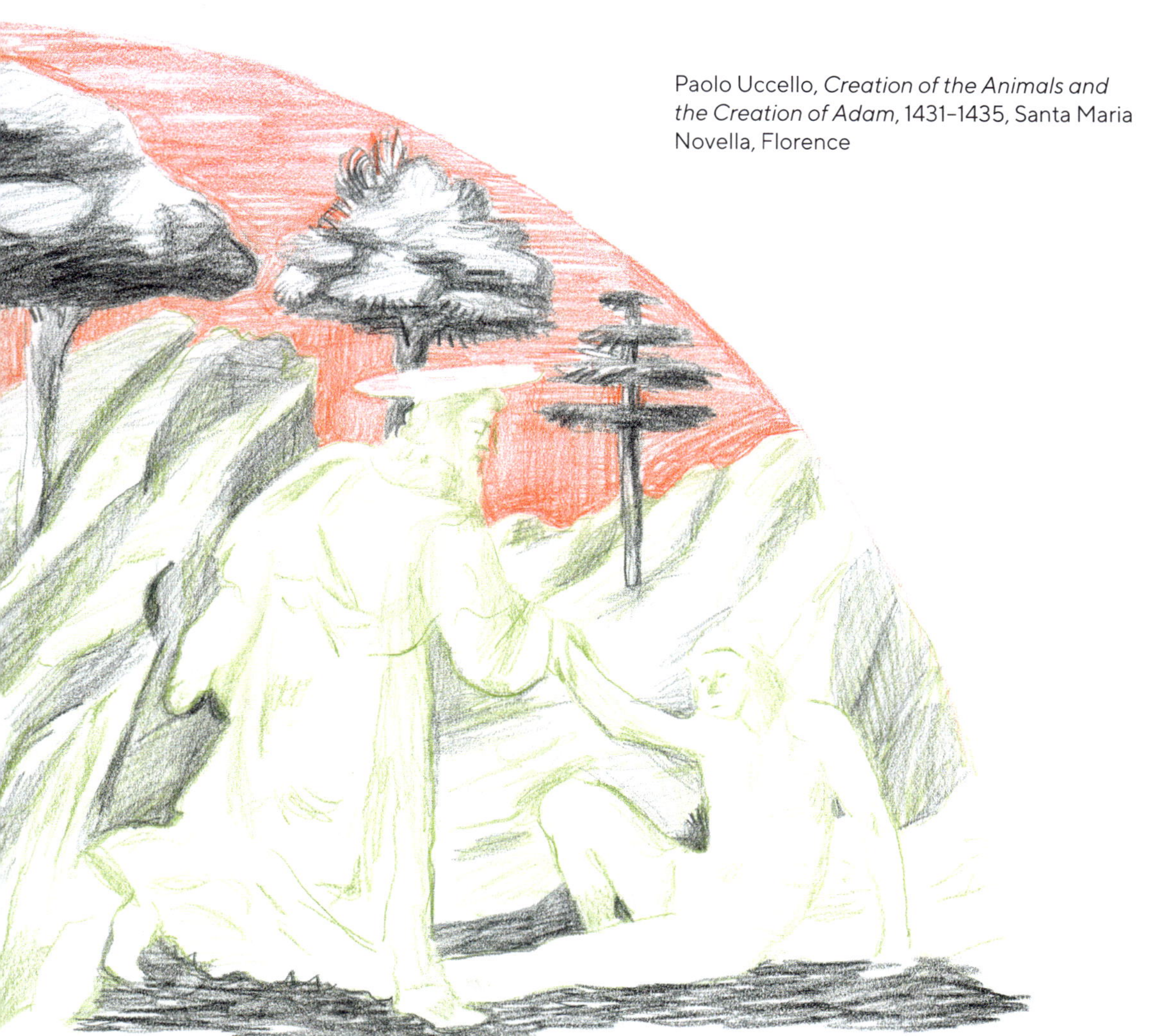

Paolo Uccello, *Creation of the Animals and the Creation of Adam*, 1431–1435, Santa Maria Novella, Florence

Complete the Creation
Try to work out which animals the painter depicts and then add any others you wish in the part of the fresco that is no longer visible at present.

THE SIGNIFICANCE OF GREEN CLOTHING

In many old paintings, artists have chosen green for the garments of important gentlemen and gentlewomen. A good example is this portrait of Signora Arnolfini, the wife of a very wealthy merchant from Lucca who emigrated to Bruges on business. This rich 15th-century lady was painted with her husband in her bridal chamber, wearing a dress of soft, shiny green. Her dress is full and elegant, with an abundance of folds and fur trimmings; the color reminds us of a spring meadow about to bloom, just like love of this married couple.

Jan van Eyck, *The Arnolfini Marriage*, 1434, National Gallery, London

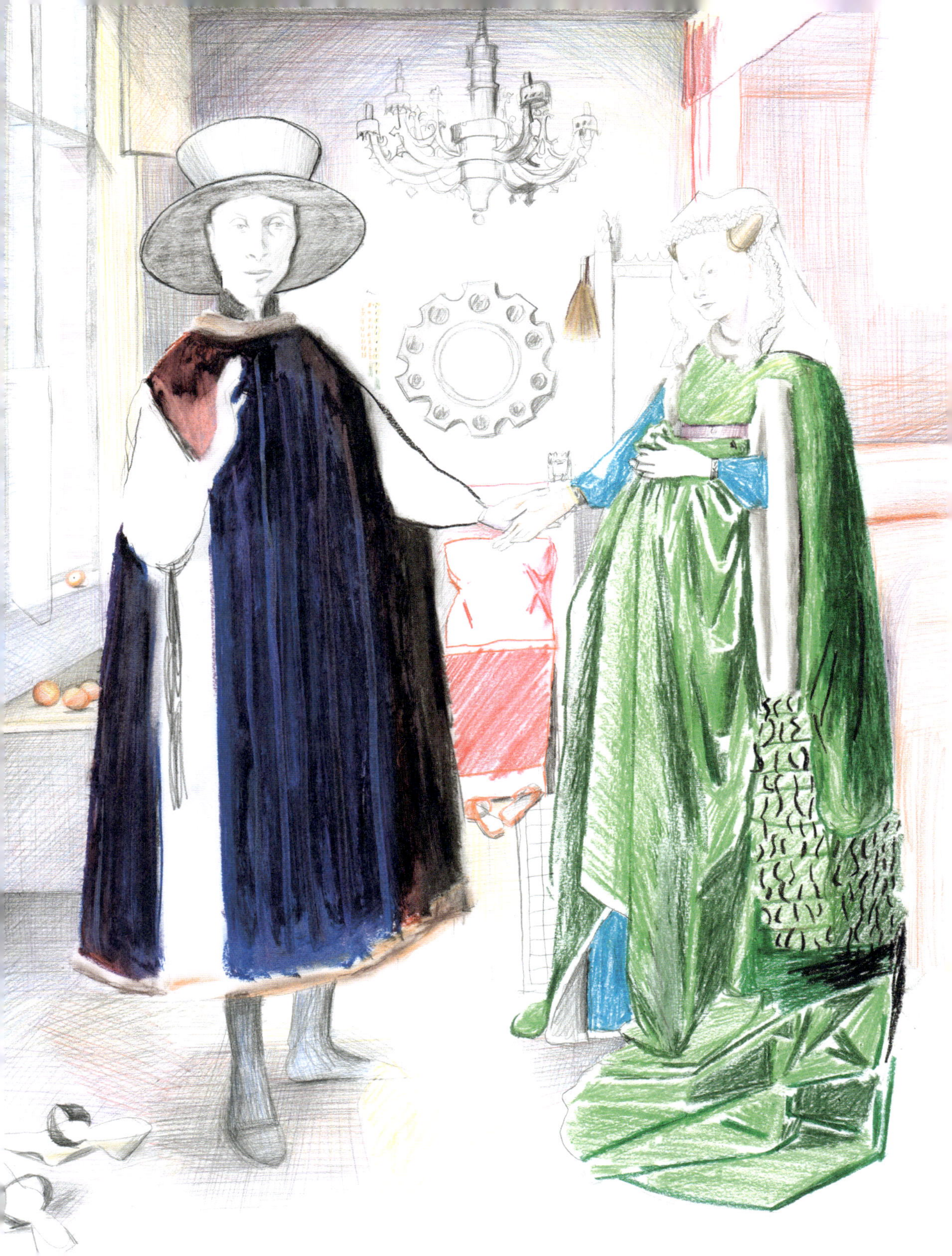

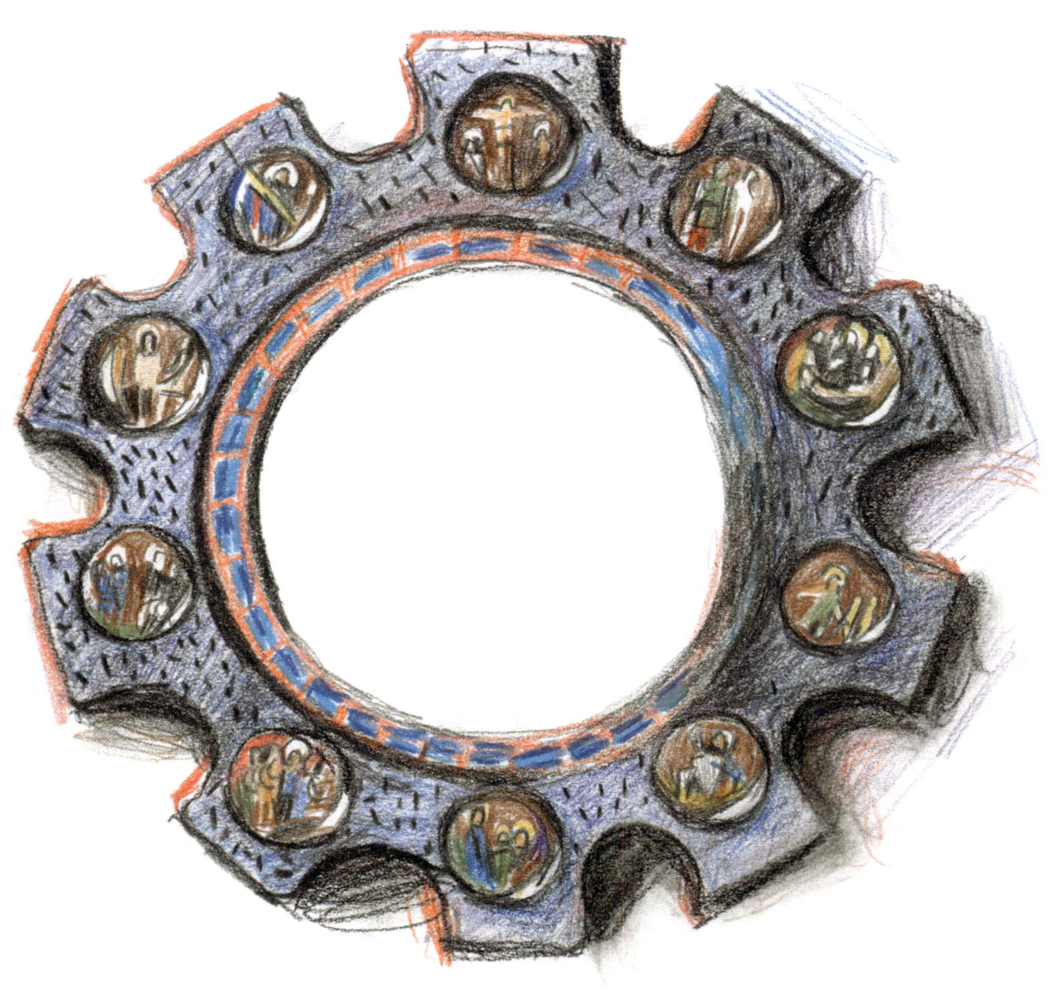

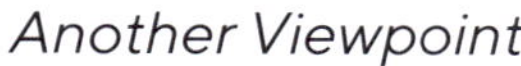

Another Viewpoint

All the details in the Van Eyck painting are executed with extraordinary precision and have a specific symbolic meaning; among these, the most famous detail is the small, convex mirror in the background that reflects the scene from the viewpoint opposite to ours. A clear mirror denotes piety, reinforced by the images of the passion of Christ on the frame. Try imagining and drawing what it reflects below.

MODERN STYLE

Another beautiful green dress is worn by a young and elegant lady portrayed by a highly skilled Polish painter who, throughout her life, traveled the world and became not only a famous artist but also a baroness. The outfit painted by Tamara de Lempicka is the latest fashion, billowing and refined. It looks sculpted and yet it's as light as paper.

Softness and Folds
Art of this quality demands skill, patience and endless practice. Prepare a selection of brushes and green watercolors and try to reproduce the folds of a silk blouse. Try to give it the kind of lightness you see in the Lempicka portrait.

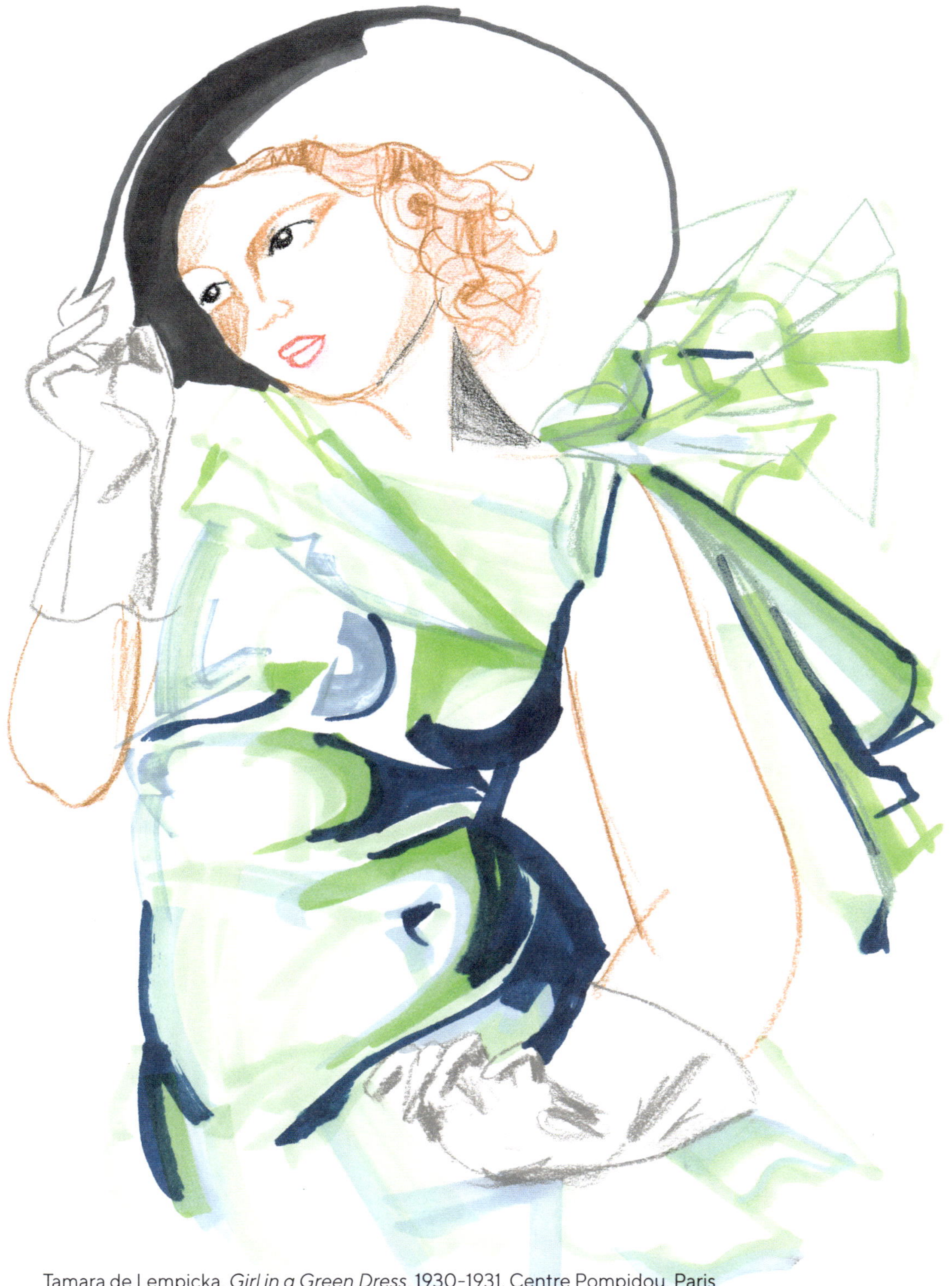

Tamara de Lempicka, *Girl in a Green Dress*, 1930–1931, Centre Pompidou, Paris

A FAIRY RING

Green is also worn by forest fairies, creatures ready to hide and camouflage themselves in the grass, leaves and trees, much loved in northern European countries where they feature in fairy tales and legends. Edward-Burne Jones was an English Pre-Raphaelite painter who was inspired by folklore, and below we can see his depiction of some forest fairies sitting in a circle in a meadow, reading, resting, and chatting, just the way we would.

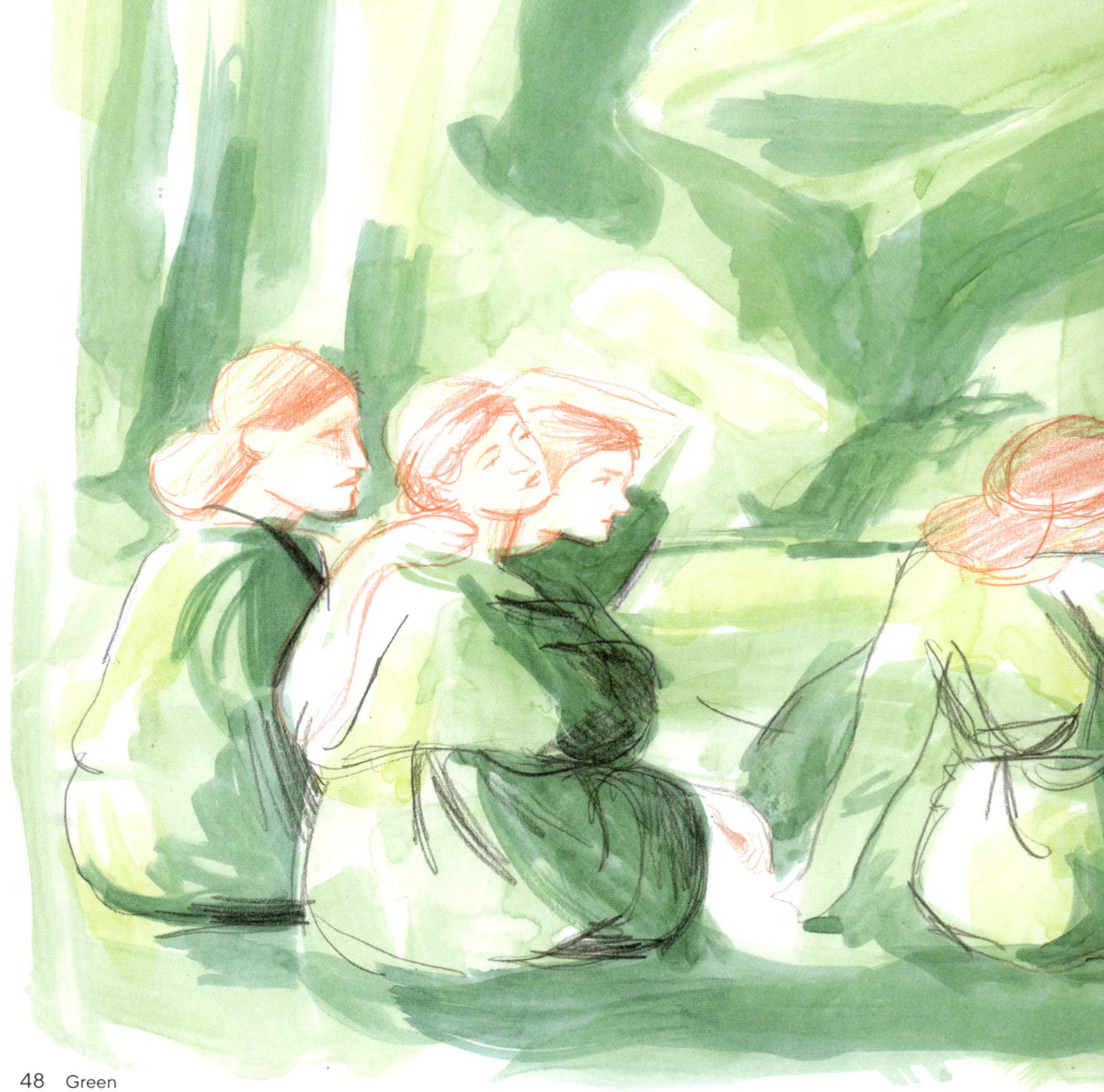

When you go walking in the woods, take with you a pencil and a notebook; take inspiration from nature and draw your own forest fairy.

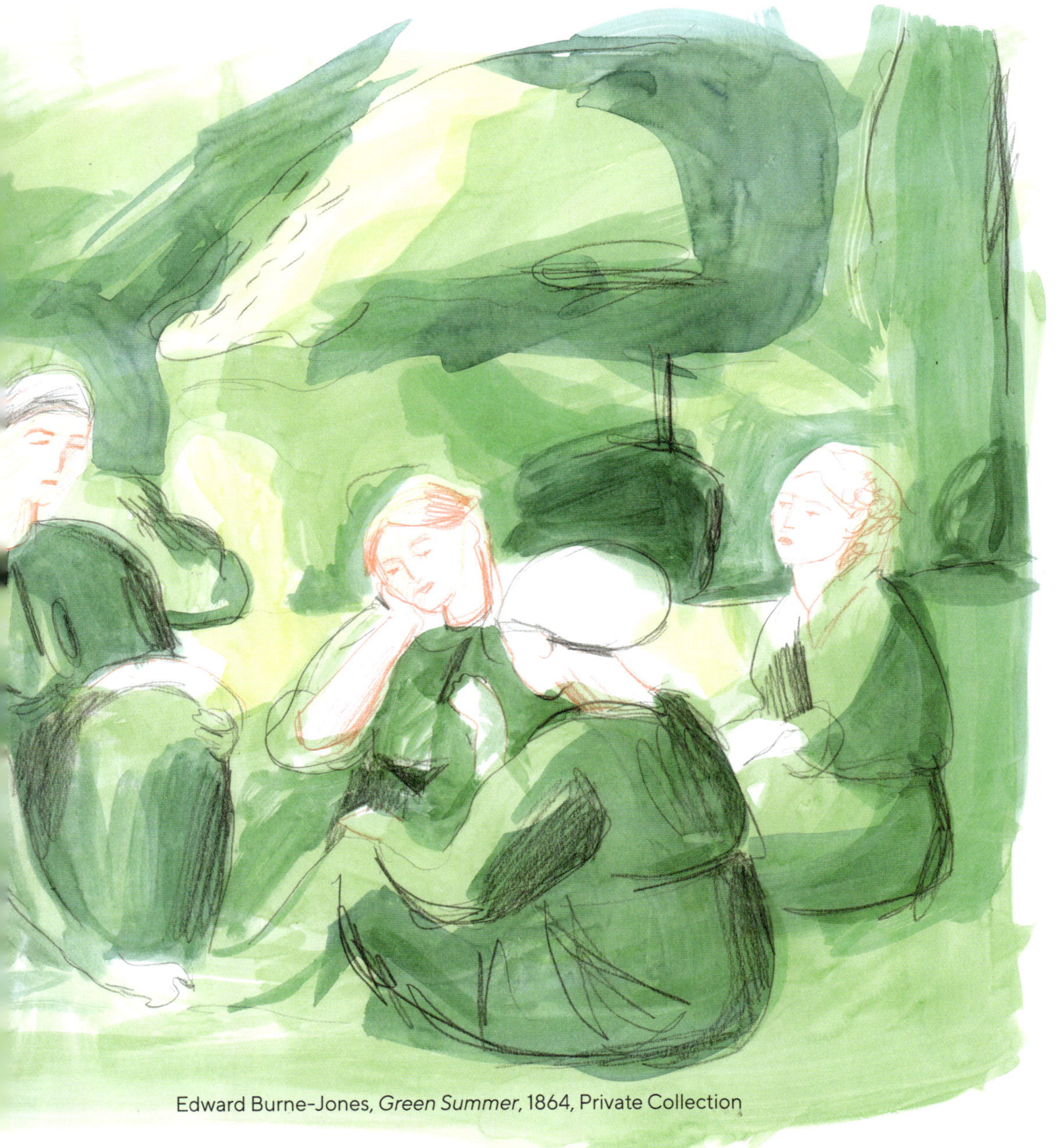

Edward Burne-Jones, *Green Summer*, 1864, Private Collection

THE PARTY IN GREEN

The painter Paolo Veronese used a glorious green in his paintings, obtained through mixing verdigris, frequently used at that time, with a particular kind of yellow. This tone was so special that when, much later, an artificial color of a similar shade was created, it was called Paolo Veronese green.

One of his most famous paintings depicts Jesus's first miracle or the Marriage at Cana, at which water was turned into wine. It is a huge canvas, an extraordinary feast for the eyes. Look at all the details: the food, the dishes, the rich green of the clothes, and even the posture of the guests and the animals. There is even a small green parrot: can you see it?

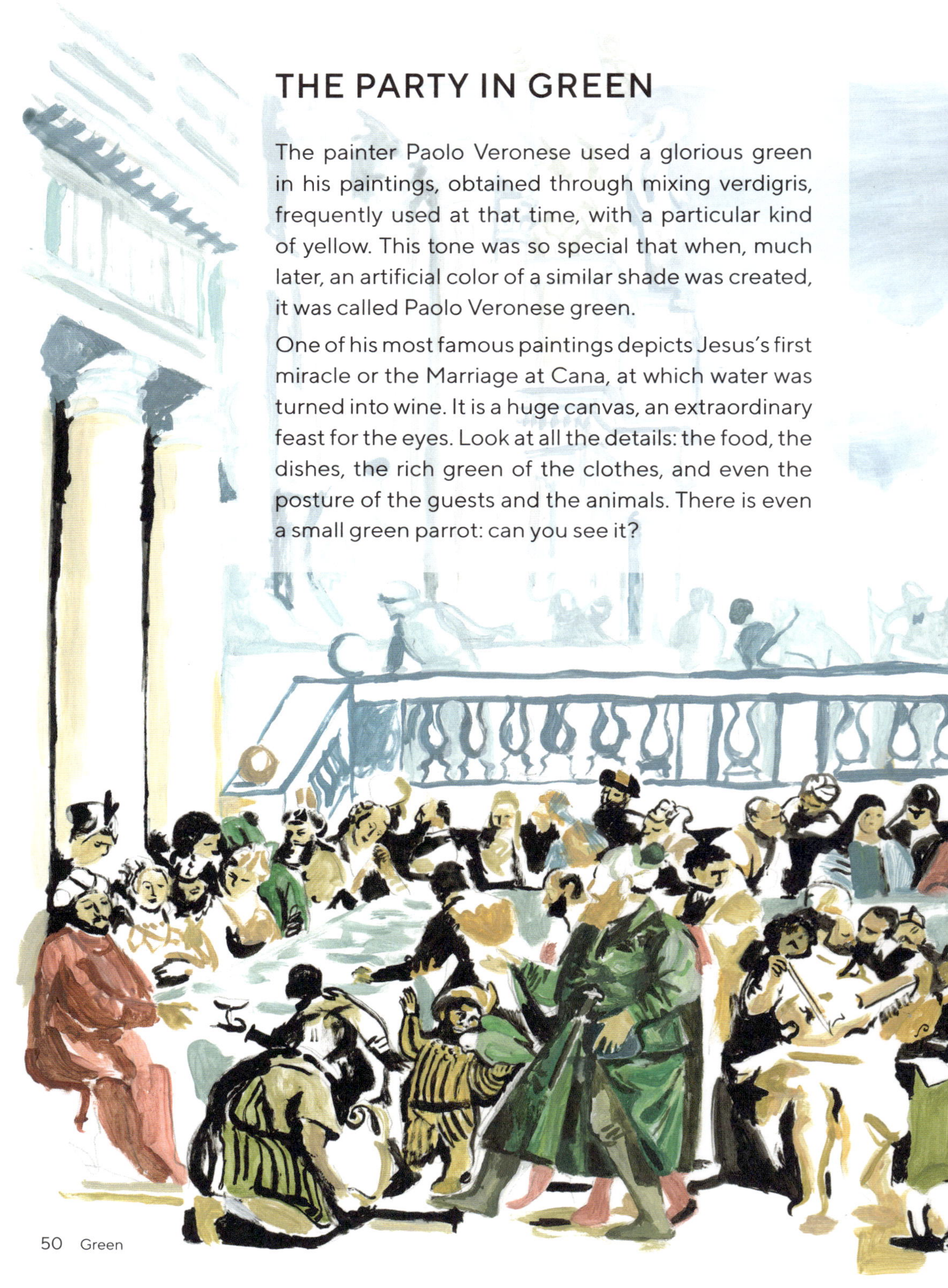

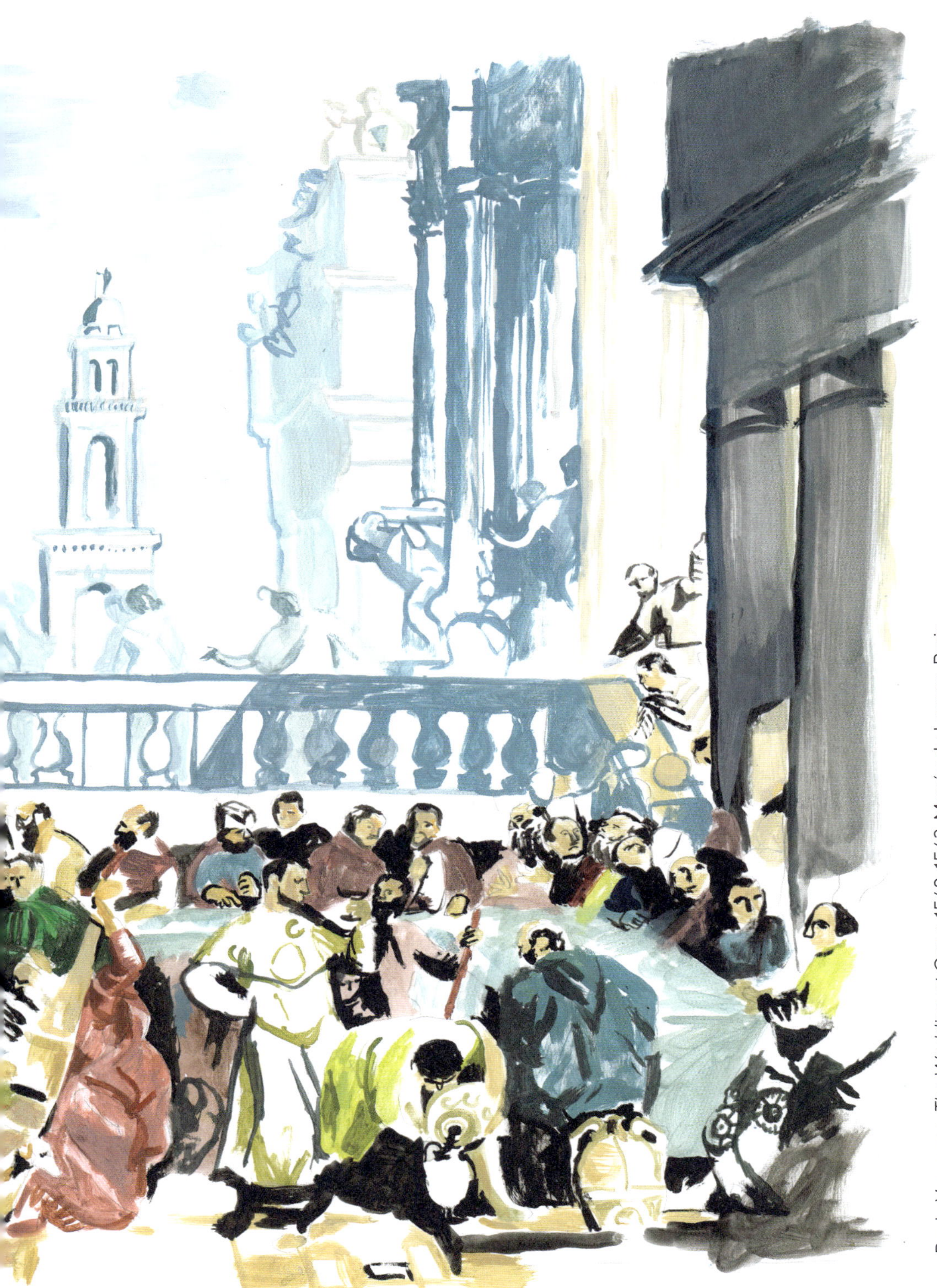

Paolo Veronese, *The Wedding at Cana*, 1562–1563, Musée du Louvre, Paris

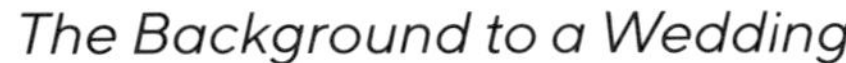

The Background to a Wedding

Imagine you're at a wedding. Sketch in the general background in green, then populate the room with guests. You may want to keep a green theme. It can be large gathering, as in the Veronese painting, or just a select few.

MEDIEVAL FACE LIFT

Rather than being a feature of the paintings, medieval European artists, on the other hand, would conceal green under the skin of their characters. It was their secret: in order to paint faces, they would spread a brown-green concoction, called verdaccio, over the painting surface, over which they would then apply very fine strokes of pink. That way, faces acquired a more natural aspect, at the same time giving the skin depth and luminosity. If you look carefully at the faces of Giotto's characters, for example, you will notice verdaccio showing through the rosy cheeks, forehead, and neck.

Skin Tones

Look at yourself in the mirror and try to mix a flesh color to match your skin tones. For a Caucasian skin, do as Cennino Cennini, the painting master, suggested: make three different shades of pink by mixing red and white in varying quantities.

Giotto, *Ognissanti Madonna*, 1303–1305, Uffizi Gallery, Florence

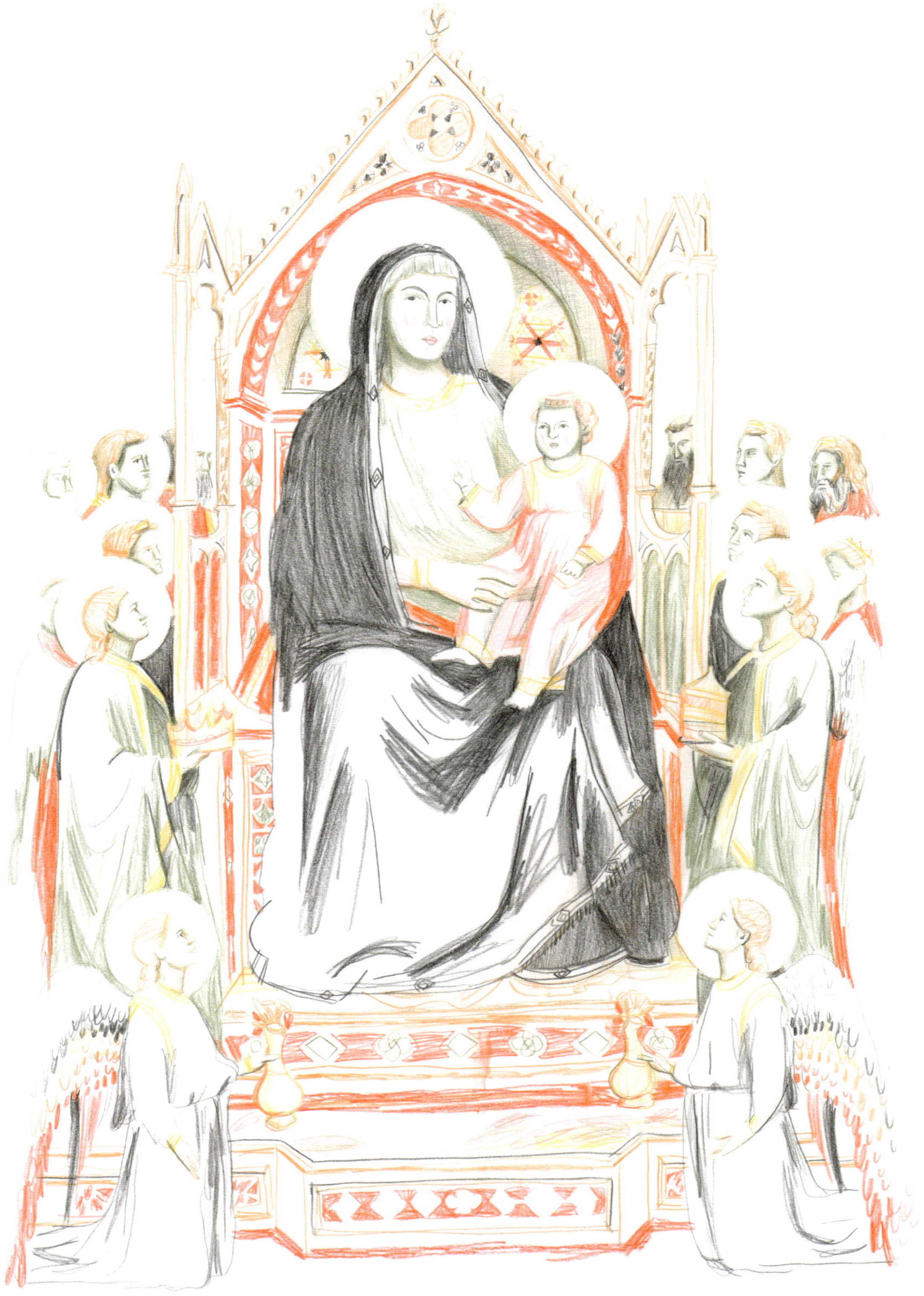

Self Portrait

Paint your portrait below using the skin color you have created using the paler or darker pink for the light and shade on the face. You could incorporate the smallest hint of green to make the color more accurate. For a darker skin coloring, you will still find that a touch of green with brown and white will help to mix a correct skin tone.

When you are happy with your own skin tones, investigate other ethnicities.

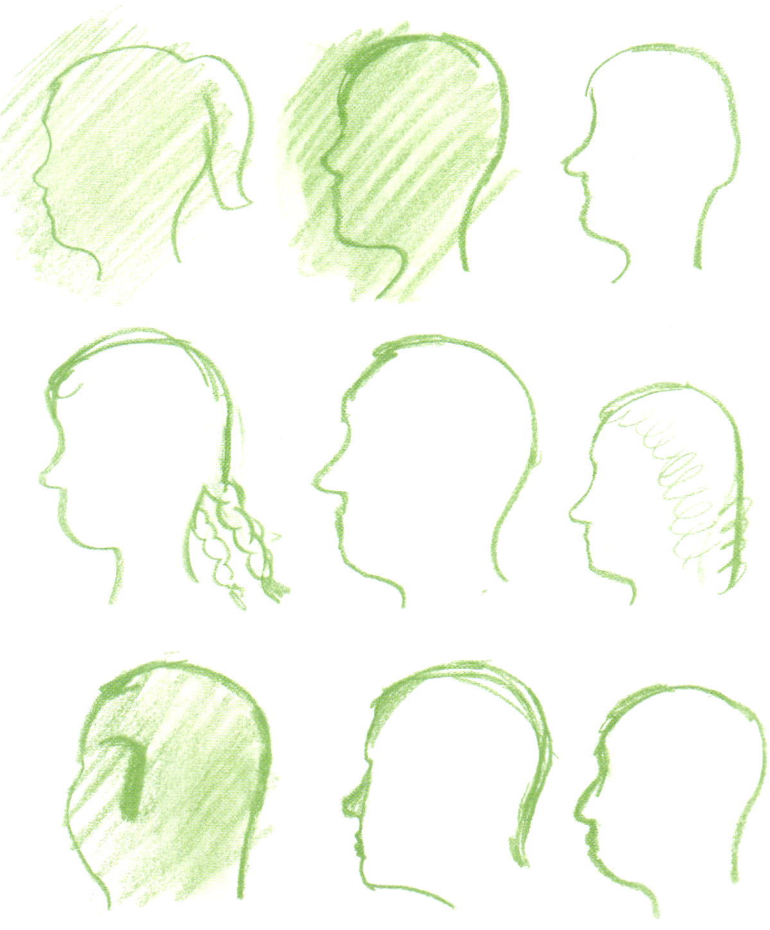

MERGING COLORS

The French artist Georges Seurat was fascinated by color. He knew that colors tend to merge in our brain and decided to use a trick: to give the impression of a green field, he had fun juxtaposing short strokes of blue over the green where the field was in the shade, and short yellow strokes where the field was in the sunlight. If you look closely at his paintings, they are made up of tiny dots of color but from a distance, the colors blend in your vision. The style is called pointillism.

Use this style to fill in the figures and background in the painting overleaf. In the shady areas, make small yellow and blue marks close together, then put the sheet of paper as far away from you as possible. As though by magic, the dots will merge and the area will appear green. Try it with various combinations of colors to complete the picture.

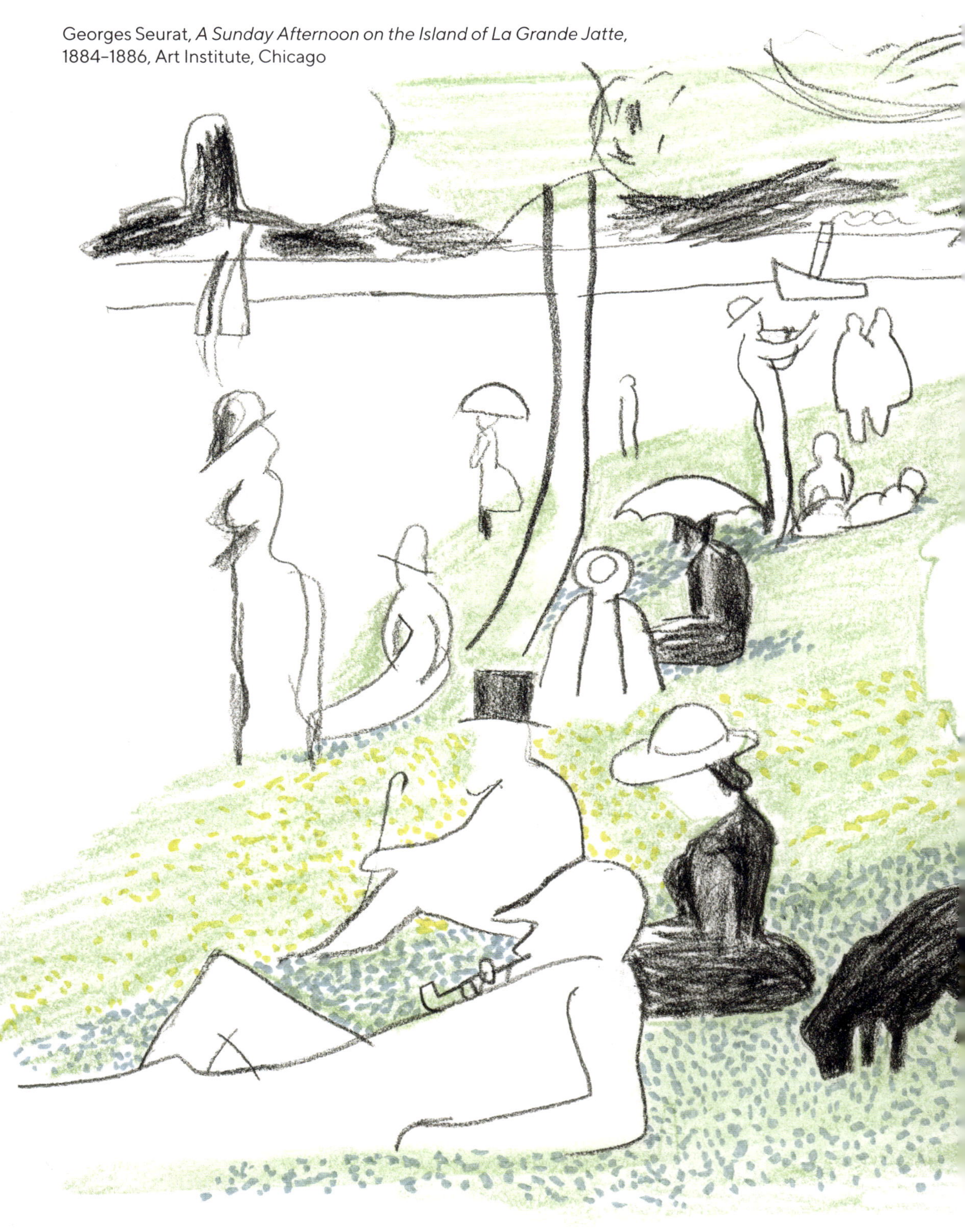

Georges Seurat, *A Sunday Afternoon on the Island of La Grande Jatte*, 1884–1886, Art Institute, Chicago

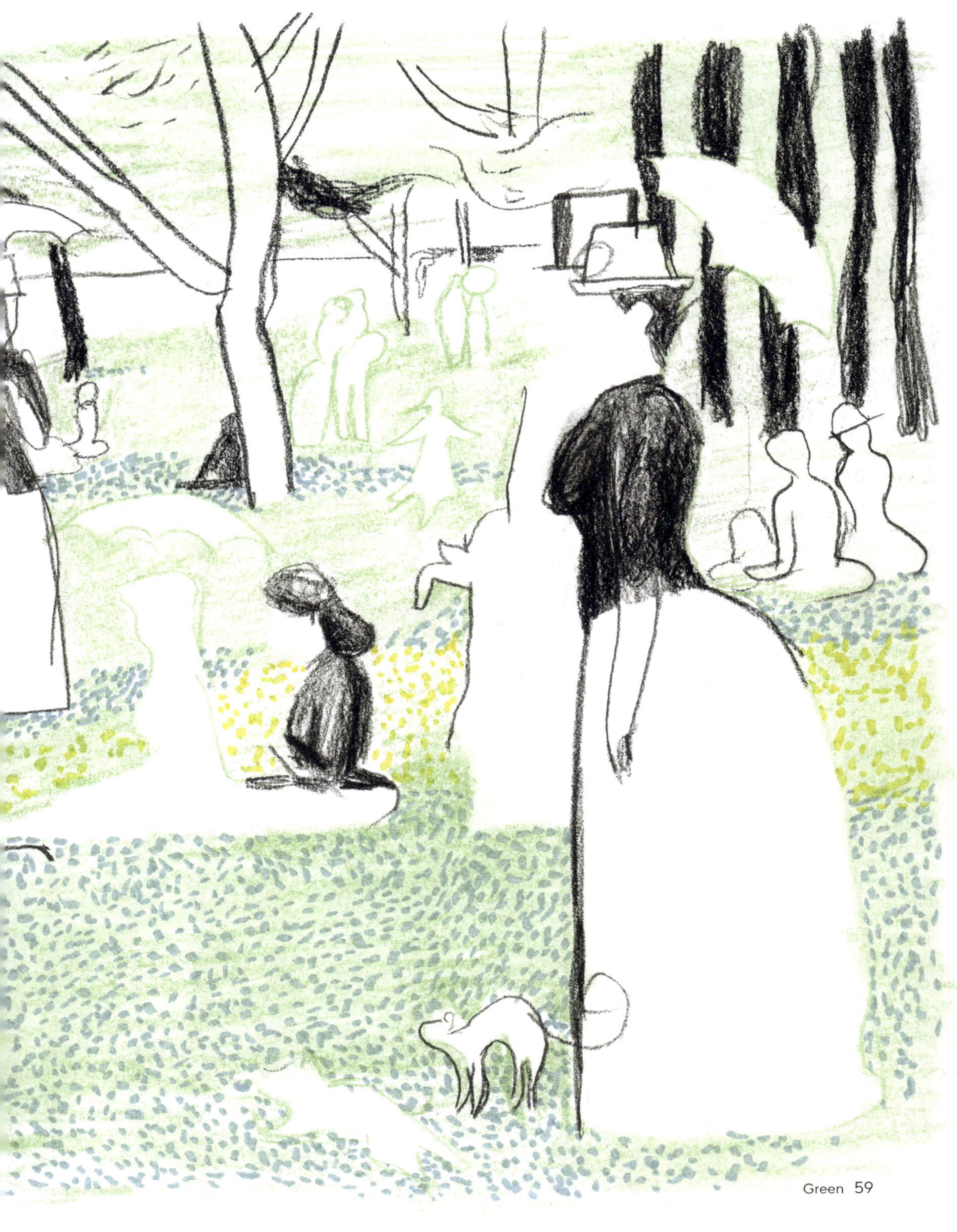

GREEN ALL AROUND YOU

Now that this book is drawing to its conclusion, try to think of how many green things you know and make a list: from pale, pistachio green to vibrant green mint. From sour limes to warm fall leaves. From intense emeralds to the phosphorescent Martians of our imagination. Green is considered the ultimate color of nature, of cleanliness, of freshness and of health. But petrol and banknotes are also green, as are creatures in stories like *Peter Pan*, witches with green teeth and eyes, and tiny forest elves. Green is associated with luck and hope. Think about the emotions this color triggers in you and what meanings you can associate it with. Use the space below to draw some green objects in your house.

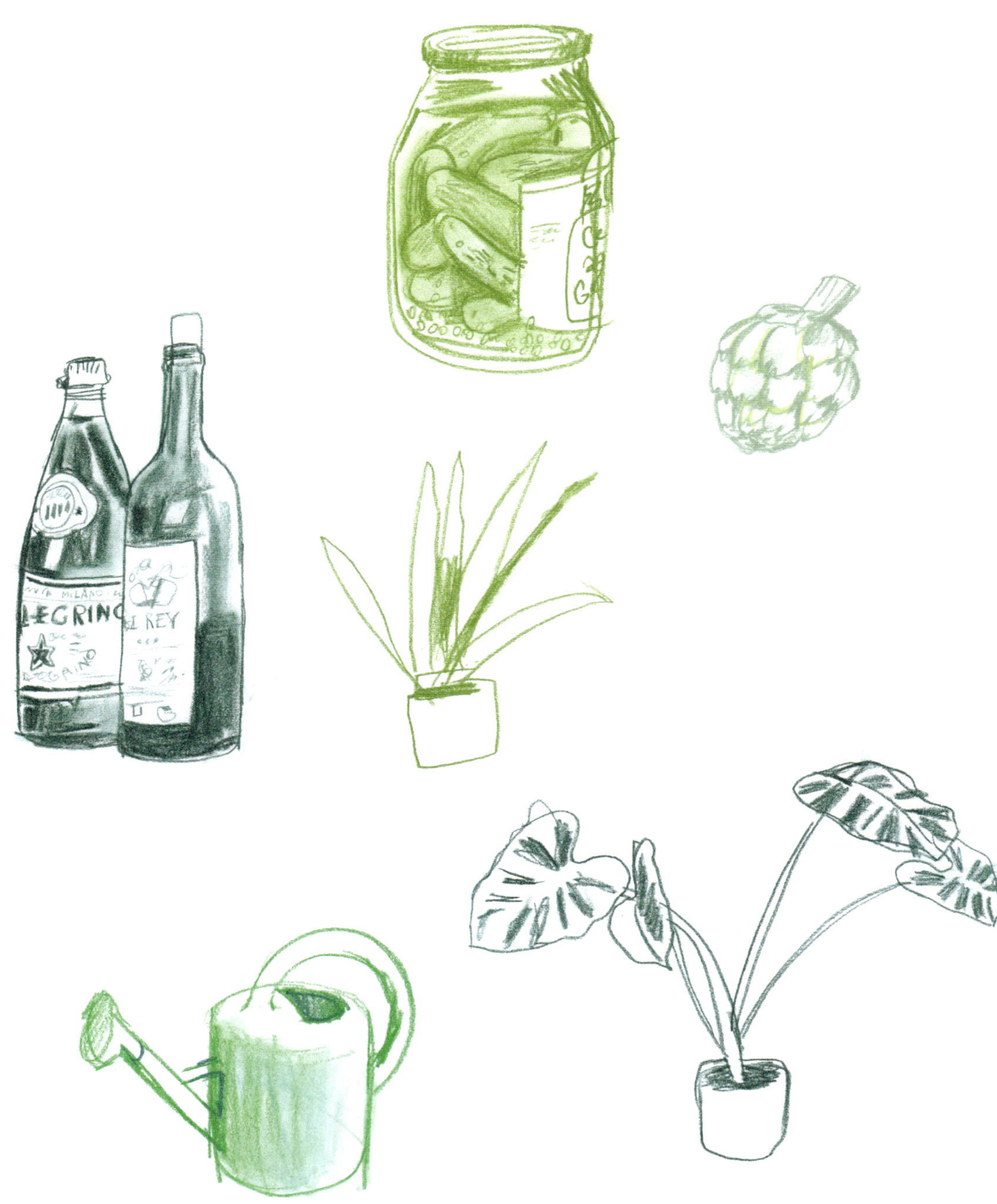

WHERE TO FIND OUT MORE

There is an infinite resource of images and information on the internet just waiting to be discovered. Here are just a few places you might start to find out more about some of the pieces of artwork in this book.

Courtauld Institute Galleries, London, courtauld.ac.uk

Denver Art Museum, denverartmuseum.org

Galerie Beyeler, Basel, fondationbeyeler.ch/en/

Hermitage Museum, Saint Petersburg, hermitagemuseum, org

Musée d'Orsay, Paris, m.musee-orsay.fr/en/home.html

Musée Marmottan, Paris, marmottan.fr/en/

Museum of Modern Art, New York, moma.org

National Gallery, London, nationalgallery.org.uk

Palazzo Vecchio, Florence, florence-museum.com/palazzo-vecchio.php

Uffizi, Florence, uffizi.it/en/the-uffiz

Anselm Keifer (b1945) German painter and sculptor working in mixed media including clay and straw.

Benvenuto Cellini (1500–1543) Italian artist and poet.

Cennino Cellini (c1360–1427) Italian painter and author of a handbook of painting.

Claude Monet (1840–1926) One of the founders of the Impressionist movement in Paris, an artist who spent a lifetime studying the effects of light.

Henri Rousseau (1844–1910) Self-taught French artist who only gave up his job as a tax collector to paint full time at the age of 49, his post-Impressionist style was known as Primitive.

Jacopo Ligozzi (1547–1627) Late Renaissance painter and illustrator.

Paolo Uccello (c1397–1475) Florentine painter and mathematician who explored the concept of perspective in his art.

Paulo Veronese (1528–1588) Italian Renaissance painter known for his huge historical and religious paintings.

Ulisse Aldrovandi (1522–1605) Naturalist, the impetus behind the Bologna botanical gardens, one of the first in Europe.

Paul Cézanne (1839–1906) French Post-Impressionist whose work formed the foundation of the development of abstract art.

Ridolfo del Ghirlandaio (1483–1561) Italian Renaissance painter from a family of artists, the most famous being his father, Domenico.

ACKNOWLEDGEMENTS:

The Italian publishers would like to thank MUS.E and Giotto FILA, who
partnered with them to make these books possible.

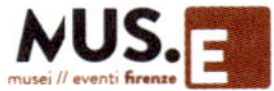 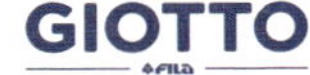

This English language edition Published in 2021 by OH!,
an imprint of Welbeck Non-Fiction Limited,
part of Welbeck Publishing Group
20 Mortimer Street
London W1T 3JW
English Translation by © Welbeck Non-Fiction Limited

First published by © Topipittori Milan in 2018
Original title: *Verde*
www.topipittori.it

Disclaimer:

Green by Valentina Zucchi and Angela Leon
ISBN 978-1-80069-059-2

Text © Valentina Zucchi and Angela Leon
Translator: Katherine Gregor
Editorial: Wendy Hobson
Design: Nikki Ellis
Production: Rachel Burgess

A CIP catalogue record for this book is available from the British Library

Printed and bound in China by Leo Paper Products Ltd.

10 9 8 7 6 5 4 3 2 1